CONFERENCE IN A BOOK™

presents

CONNECT LEAD SUCCEED

BOOK 2

THE ESSENTIALS OF LEADERSHIP AND AI FOR THE DIGITAL AGE

This book is produced as a joint initiative with the Virtual Speakers Association International. All the authors are members of that association, which is a subsidiary of the Global Speakers Federation.

If you would like to know more about the VSAI, its members or events, please visit: *www.vsainternational.org*

First Published 2026 by Indie Experts Publishing

Published by Indie Experts Publishing & Author Services

Copyright © Indie Experts Publishing

Disclaimer:
Every effort has been made to ensure this book is as accurate and complete as possible, however they may be errors both typographical and in content. The author and the publisher shall not be held liable or responsible to any person or entity with respect to any loss or damage caused or alleged to have been caused directly or indirectly by the information contained in this book. Some names and identifying details in this book have been changed to protect the privacy of individuals.

Curated by Dixie Maria Carlton
www.indieexpertspublishing.com

Cover design and typesetting by
Ammie Christiansen, Fast Forward Design
www.fastforwarddesign.co.nz

Typeset in 11pt Minion Pro

ISBN:

978-1-0671319-8-2 (Printed)
978-1-0671319-9-9   (eBook)

Dedication:

For the leaders who choose integrity over convenience, courage over comfort, and people over performance metrics.

This book is for you —
and for what you're building next.

CONTENTS

Welcome

BY DIXIE MARIA CARLTON

Book two in the Conference in a Book™ Series

Welcome to **Connect, Lead, Succeed Book 2**

Imagine this book as the opening moments of a one-day conference.

The room is filling. Conversations are warming up. Coffee cups are in hand. There's an energy in the air — not the buzz of hype, but the quiet anticipation that today might actually matter.

This is not a conference about trends for trend's sake.
And it's not a book about theory divorced from reality.

Connect, Lead, Succeed exists because leadership today is being asked to stretch — in depth, in responsibility, and in capability — at a pace few of us were prepared for.

A Note on the Series

Connect, Lead, Succeed is not a single conversation — it's a continuing one.

Book 1 established the foundations: connection, communication, confidence, culture, and the human skills that allow leaders to build trust, influence others, and create momentum. It explored what it takes to lead *with* people — not over them — in environments shaped by change, complexity, and competing priorities.

Book 2 builds on that groundwork and moves the conversation forward.

Here, we deepen the leadership lens and expand capability. We explore what happens when strong human leadership meets accelerating technology — and why the inner work of leadership matters more, not less, in an AI-enabled world. Together, these two volumes form a complete conference experience: from connection to capability, from mindset to method, from leadership presence to scalable impact.

Read individually, each book stands on its own. Read together, they tell a bigger story — one about how leaders evolve, adapt, and stay human while shaping the future.

The Leadership Conversation

We begin where every meaningful conference should begin: with leadership.

Not leadership as performance or position, but leadership as a lived practice — shaped in moments of uncertainty, ethical tension, human connection, and decision-making under pressure.

The leadership chapters in this book invite you to slow down before you speed up. To look inward before you scale outward. To examine how courage, self-awareness, dialogue, friction, and trust show up in your leadership — not in theory, but in real life.

These voices explore leadership as something embodied, not declared. Something built over time, not downloaded overnight. And something that carries weight — because leadership always leaves a legacy, whether we intend it to or not.

This section sets the tone for everything that follows. Because without clarity of leadership, no tool — no matter how powerful — will create meaningful impact.

The AI Conversation

Then the conversation shifts.

The tools arrive.
The pace quickens.
And the question becomes one of capability.

Artificial Intelligence is no longer waiting in the wings. It's already integrated into how we write, decide, communicate, analyse, and scale. And yet, for many leaders, the conversation around AI is still clouded by noise — hype on one side, fear on the other.

It's also timely to refer to AI as 'Assisted' Intelligence, because this section brings AI back into the realm of practical leadership.

Not as a replacement for thinking, but as a partner to it.

Not as a shortcut, but as leverage.

Not as an answer, but as an amplifier of intent.

The chapters that follow explore how AI can extend human capacity — when guided by clear leadership, ethical judgment, and purposeful application. They invite you to think critically about where AI belongs, where it doesn't, and how to stay firmly in the driver's seat as the tools evolve.

Because AI doesn't lead.

People do.

The Invitation

This book is not meant to be skimmed like a manual. It's meant to be experienced like a conference you're fully present for.

Some chapters will challenge you.
Some will ground you.

Some will spark new ways of thinking about your role as a leader, a professional, and a human navigating rapid change.

My invitation to you is simple:

Read with intention.
Pause when something resonates.
Notice what shifts — not just in how you think, but in how you lead.

So take a breath.
Find your seat.
And stay curious.

Welcome to **Connect, Lead, Succeed Book 2** —where leadership meets capability, and the future is shaped with purpose. So take a breath.

Turn the page.

The day is about to begin.

— Dixie Carlton
Founder, Indie Experts Publishing
Global Author Coach & Strategist
Executive Producer of the "Conference in a Book"™ Series

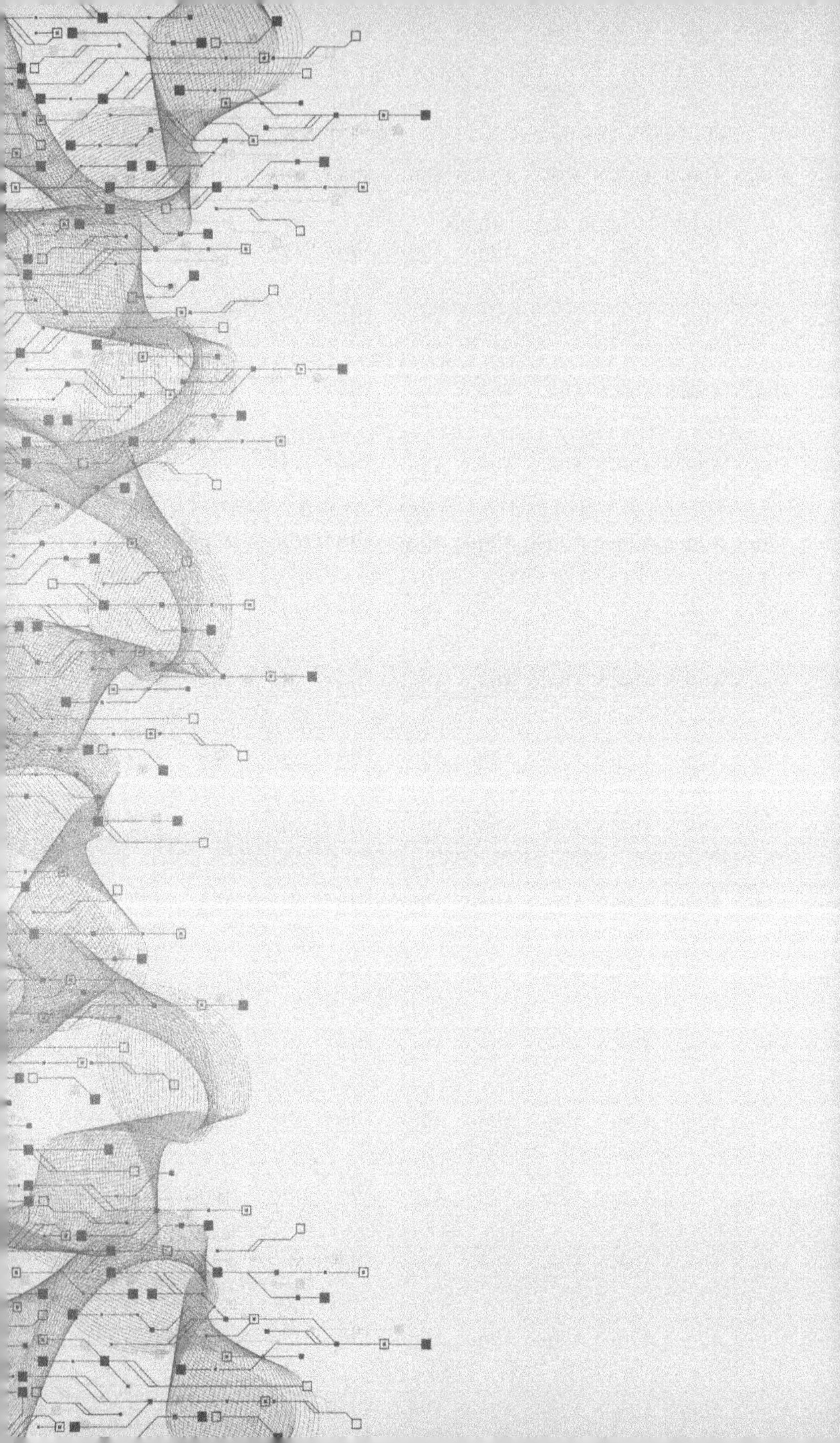

SESSION ONE

Leadership

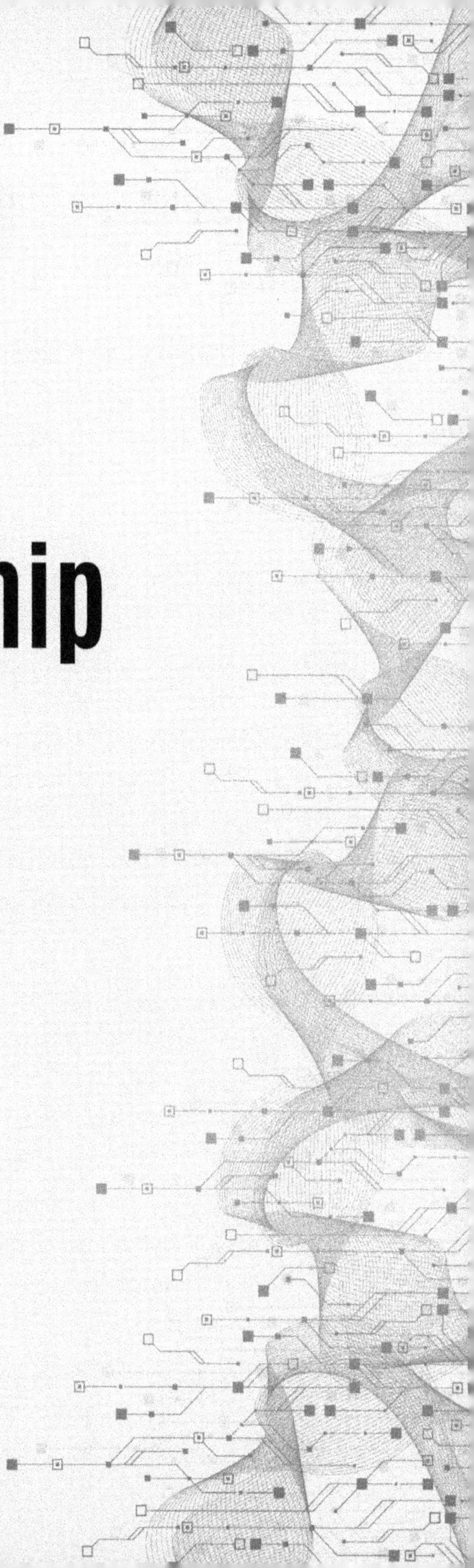

Harriet L. Russell

Kim Liddell

Sarah Morse

Dr Suresh Verghis

Claudia Cimenti

Browyn Reid

Ravin Papiah

Leadership: Where It All Begins (Again)

If this book is a one-day conference, then the Leadership section is where we gather first — not because leadership is the loudest topic in the room, but because it sets the tone for everything that follows.

Before we talk about systems, strategy, culture, technology, or growth, we must talk about who is leading — and how.

Leadership today is no longer defined by authority, position, or certainty. It is shaped in moments of ambiguity, pressure, and responsibility. It is tested when answers are incomplete, when tension rises, and when the easy option is not the right one. And increasingly, leadership is lived not on stages or in titles, but in conversations, decisions, and the quiet courage to act with integrity.

This section opens the conference by going inward before moving outward.

The chapters that follow explore leadership as a human practice — one that begins with self-awareness and expands into courage, trust, dialogue, friction, and responsibility. These are not theoretical models or idealised versions of leadership. They are lived experiences, forged in real environments where the consequences matter.

You'll meet leaders who invite us to slow down and reconnect with our inner compass. Leaders who challenge us to act when doing nothing would be easier. Leaders who show us that conversations shape culture, that friction can be productive, and that courage compounds over time.

Together, these voices remind us that leadership is not about having all the answers — it's about being willing to stay present in the questions.

This section is not designed to be consumed passively. Like the opening sessions of a powerful conference, it asks something of you. Reflection. Honesty. Willingness. A readiness to notice where your leadership is aligned — and where it might be asking for recalibration.

So take a seat.

Set your intention.

This is where the day truly begins.

Turn the page — and step into the leadership conversation.

Our first chapter invites us to slow down, turn inward, and reconsider where leadership really begins. Not in strategy decks or org charts, but in self-awareness, alignment, and the quiet intelligence that lives beneath words.

Introducing Harriet L. Russell, USA

Harriet *brings a lifetime of global experience to this conversation — from working on Wall Street to deep cultural immersion in Japan — and she challenges us to lead from the inside out. Drawing on timeless Japanese concepts such as intuition, preparation, and interdependence, Harriet reframes leadership as something we embody, not perform.*

This is not a chapter about being louder, faster, or more visible. It's about becoming more grounded, more intentional, and more human.

So as you read, I invite you to do more than absorb ideas. Pause. Reflect. Notice what resonates.

Because the most powerful leadership journey you'll ever take is the one that leads you home to yourself.

Know Thyself: Leading from the Inside Out

Leadership is not about titles or tasks. It's about personal truth and self-awareness.

Why Leadership Starts Within

In a world full of credentials, techniques, and certifications, we often chase the next thing to make ourselves better leaders. Yet, the real power of leadership doesn't come from what's on our résumé — it comes from who we are at our core.

I've worked on Wall Street, lived in Japan, taught personal development, and run my own business. What I've learned across these different worlds is that leadership is not about titles or tasks. It's about personal truth and self-awareness.

You can teach someone financial modeling. You can train someone in presentation skills. But you cannot teach someone how to be aligned with their authentic self. That's something each of us must discover — and leadership must begin there.

Know Thyself: The True Foundation of Leadership

We live in a world that rewards the cosmetic: degrees, memberships, board seats, and polished LinkedIn bios. But these are just decorations. Real leadership is about understanding your own strengths and limitations — your pluses and minuses — so you can operate from a place of self-awareness rather than performing according to others' expectations.

I once applied for a senior leadership role with a German company overseeing a Japanese business unit. I didn't have an MBA, and the interviewer made a point of noting it. I replied, "An MBA teaches valuable business fundamentals. What I bring is years of cultural fluency and lived experience in Japan. That can't be learned in a classroom."

I convinced the German CEO that, in contrast to typical Western leadership training — which is often centered on communication techniques, team dynamics, and strategic planning — my time in Japan had focused on cultivating the inner self and that when you understand and refine who you are at your core, your ability to lead others, shape strategy, and manage the "nuts and bolts" of a company naturally strengthens.

They hired me.

During several years living in Japan, I discovered a deeper dimension of leadership. The Japanese had a language for what I had long intuited: *haragei* — trusting your gut and listening beyond words; *nemawashi* — quietly building alignment and consensus before action; and *amae* — allowing connection and interdependence. These are not exotic cultural concepts but universal practices for leadership maturity. They remind us that knowing yourself is inseparable from knowing how to move with others.

Skills can always be acquired. The crucial question is this: *Do you truly know who you are — and are you leading from that place of alignment?*

Learning from Japan: Energy, Alignment, and Quiet Influence

In Western culture, leadership is often measured by action, output, and titles. Yet the Japanese lens recognizes another dimension — one that harmonizes beautifully with the idea of energy gain versus energy drain.

- **Haragei** reminds us that leadership is not always loud or performative. True influence often comes from presence, intuition, and the energy we radiate. By practicing silence and reading between the lines, we conserve energy rather than scattering it.

- **Nemawashi** teaches us that groundwork matters. Instead of rushing decisions or chasing recognition, we prepare patiently, aligning with ourselves first, then with others. This quiet investment prevents energy drain later.

- **Amae** reminds us that leadership is not solitary. Allowing ourselves to lean on others creates strength through connection. We don't need to burn out proving independence; instead, interdependence sustains energy and builds trust.

For Western leaders, the lesson is clear: success is not found in titles, noise, or overextension. It is found in knowing what fuels you, preparing thoughtfully, and leading through authentic presence and shared humanity.

Leadership is not "power over." It is "power with," guided by energy, patience, and connection.

First I came to appreciate the practice of haragei — literally, the "art of the belly." It's not about clever words or polished credentials, but about the presence you carry and the energy others feel from you. Silence, timing, and intuition matter as much as speech. Haragei reminds us that influence comes not only from what we say, but also from who we are beneath the surface.

腹芸

Haragei – The Art of Business Negotiation

In Japan, it is important to be in touch with your intuition and gut instincts. This is called haragei, or the Art of Hara — a way of being beyond the mind. Hara means "belly," your "honorable middle," the center of your physical body. It is what grounds you. It is your source, the navel center, where all your vital organs are. It is where the most important connection resides. The art of hara is about drawing deep power from your center, accessing a sense of confidence and calm. Haragei relates to charisma and strength of presence.

I witnessed one of the most profound displays of silence and haragei in 1992. I arranged for my yoga guru, Yogi Amrit Desai, from the U.S., to conduct a seminar tour in Japan. One morning at 5 a.m., I took him to meet my former martial arts master, Dōshu Kisshōmaru Ueshiba, the elderly son of the founder of aikido. I expected to translate some deep discussion between them about the spirituality of aikido and yoga. After greeting each other, they drank green tea. They sat. They breathed into their hara centers. They made eye contact. They lowered their eyes. They sat in silence. About 30 minutes later, I thanked the Aikido master with a full kneeling bow. After we left, I mentioned to my guru that I had expected them to have something to talk about. He replied, "We were communicating. We did not need to say anything."

Points to Remember about Silence in Japan

- Silence is important to show you are absorbing information.
- Haragei is about listening to your intuition and gut instincts.
- It is also about communicating nonverbally.

A Business Application Tip for Haragei

When I am on a virtual call with a client, I put myself on mute while they are speaking, so that I can fully listen to them and not be tempted to interrupt, comment, or interject a teaching at that time.

根回し

Nemawashi – Favors Are Not Forgotten in Long-Term Relationships

The roots are bound, and they last.

In Tokyo, I was on special assignment for several months, training in the nonferrous metals division of Nissho Iwai Corporation (now Sojitz Corporation).

Why was I allowed to be the first and only non-Japanese outsider to see the inner workings of Nissho Iwai?

It went back to an old favor and a giri (obligation) that was only now being repaid. Twenty years earlier, a young Japanese manager who spoke English well had been sent by Nissho Iwai to train in the London office of the German Metallgesellschaft (MG) conglomerate. Two decades later, as the head of MG's Japan Desk in New York City, I was sent to Nissho Iwai Tokyo to be trained. That obligation lasted

20 years and extended beyond the decision-makers of the time to a new generation of executives — and even across countries. So here I was in Tokyo again, where I had previously lived and worked for many years.

Following Their Lead

My mentor was the same gentleman who had gone to London for training 20 years earlier. Having a mentor is traditionally Japanese and a significant advantage. I was introduced to the Japanese *kachō* (managers) who spoke English, and I began observing their daily functions and work life. They all knew my background from my résumé. They spoke to me in English — even though I was in Japan, everyone else was Japanese, and they knew I was fluent in Japanese — for three whole weeks. Then suddenly, one day, they all switched to Japanese, and nothing was ever mentioned.

This was a testing period.

By simply following their lead, I spoke English when addressed in English and switched to Japanese only when they initiated it. This showed both respect and humility on my part. I was treated with professionalism in Nissho Iwai and became part of the company's daily life for the duration of my stay. I was exceptionally fortunate not only to learn their processes, but also to have a mentor for my questions and a network of personal Japanese friends and connections.

In another instance, a graduate teacher working for me in my yoga training school wanted to branch out and teach another style. I undertook advanced training in that style, although I had no intention of teaching it myself. I wanted to understand what they were passionate about and learn how to mentor them if needed. It wasn't about control. It was about insight. Insight is power when you're leading.

As leaders, we can apply the same practice inwardly: doing the groundwork with ourselves before we leap into action.

Let me ask you something. Have you…

- Consulted your own values?
- Looked at your own filters and prejudices?
- Tested your assumptions?
- Aligned with your deeper truth?

When we align our roots first, we trim the old to encourage smaller, newer roots. What grows above ground is far more resilient.

甘え

AMAE – The Value of Interdependence

Japanese relationships are long term. Their interdependence develops a sense of not only obligation, but also dependence rooted in deeper connection. Americans take pride in independence and the ability to succeed as an individual. For the Japanese, if you do not form dependent relationships, you do not truly relate.

After evening meetings, if not sent home by taxi, I was always taken not only to the train station but also accompanied a few stops further, if not all the way. I learned that this was not for my safety, as Tokyo is one of the safest cities in the world. Then why? I used to insist I lived there, knew my way, and could get home without their help — until a close friend replied, "You need to be more *amae*."

My independent self asked, "Why?"

He replied, "Because then you give us the opportunity to help you."

That moment taught me that it was not about my capabilities or needs, but about interconnectedness — creating interdependence and giving someone else the chance to help, needed or not.

Allowing someone else into my world simply by accepting their presence was unfamiliar, yet it was the foundation for long-term relationships built on repeated giving and receiving. This idea of mutual support reshaped how I understood connection, revealing that sometimes the most meaningful act is allowing others to care for you — even when you believe you can manage on your own.

There is also a degree of obligation in developing a relationship, and finding the right balance makes it comfortable for all.

I was introduced to Yoko Ono in the U.S. when I was the Training Director of the yoga and wellness facility where I worked. Before a trip to Japan to arrange a three-week seminar tour, Yoko provided me with her brother's contact information. He introduced me to a graphic artist and PR professional, who helped prepare my promotional materials and treated me as an honored guest at dinner.

Obligation met. Nothing more.

The degree of my relationship with Yoko Ono was minimal and not long term — I had met her only once — so the degree of the favor from her brother was naturally limited. Everyone and everything in its place.

From Self-Criticism to Self-Compassion: The Inner Dialogue of a Leader

One of the most powerful shifts a leader can make is in their inner dialogue.

Decades ago, the nonviolent communication movement taught us that violence isn't just physical — it can be emotional, verbal, or even internal.

How we resolve conflict, foster empathy, and build connection is related to expressing feelings and needs without blame—and listening deeply to others to find solutions that meet everyone's needs.

How we speak to ourselves matters just as much as how we speak to and with others.

Leaders must be aware of their own inner critic, their fears, their self-judgments. Why? Because what you haven't healed or resolved within yourself, you'll project outward. Self-awareness isn't just about being mindful of your thoughts; it's about redirecting them toward compassion and growth. This is not a flimsy "think positively," but a deep discipline that strengthens the brain — like a muscle — to see beyond negativity and fear. This discipline helps us to move into higher consciousness, especially when faced with challenges, doubts, and fear of "what if" outcomes.

> *What you haven't healed or resolved within yourself,*
> *you'll project outward.*

Redefining Leadership: It's Not a Title

Leadership doesn't begin when someone gives you a title. It begins when you take ownership of your impact — whether you have authority or not.

Some of the most powerful leaders I've seen had no official title. They weren't the loudest. They didn't stand at the front. But they influenced quietly from within — being fully present, supporting others, leading by example.

Leadership is not hierarchy.
It's not power over.
It's power with.

It's showing up with courage, clarity, and kindness.

Final Thoughts: Coming Home to Yourself

Ultimately, leadership is a return journey — to yourself.

The path is not:
Think → Do → Become.

It is:
Feel → Be → Think → Do.

When we chase action before identity, we burn out, misalign, and wonder why success feels hollow.

When we lead from the inside out, however, success is not just sustainable — it's joyful.

True leadership is not found in external accolades or the relentless pursuit of more. It resides within, a deep wellspring of self-awareness and integrity. When you lead from this place of authenticity, you don't just achieve goals — you create ripples of trust, alignment, and connection that last far beyond your own work.

You create impact as a "sensei," "guru," or teacher who shows they are a perpetual student, not of external knowledge but of internal growth through interaction with others and mirrored reflection.

My Reflection Questions for You

- What parts of your leadership journey have felt misaligned with your true self?

- What do you currently do that drains you in action and in self-talk — and what would happen if you stopped?

- Where can you delegate, collaborate more? Where can you learn more?

- What's your inner voice saying — and how can you shift it to be more supportive?

- Are you chasing titles or embracing truth? Can you authentically do both?

Leadership isn't about changing who you are.
It's about becoming more of who you were always
meant to be.

— Harriet

About Harriet

Harriet L. Russell helps people work together across cultures with greater ease, awareness, and trust. Her global career spans roles as a PR Manager at Sony in New York City, sole translator and consultant for ABC News at the 1979 G7 Tokyo Economic Summit, U.S. speaker sent by the U.S. State Dept. to Belarus, - and many other experiences that have shaped her deep understanding of cross-cultural competence.

A native of Ohio, Harriet lived overseas for many years, is fluent in several languages, and speaks at global leadership summits and business conferences worldwide. Her work has been recognized by the Fulbright Commission, Rotary International's Paul Harris Award for "creating friendly relations among peoples of the world," and through her founding of an English-language library in Kyrgyzstan. At 24, she also spent six months traveling overland through the Middle East.

After working with Harriet, leaders feel more grounded, communicate more effectively, and collaborate with confidence. She teaches leadership with authenticity, mindfulness, and respect — reducing friction while improving outcomes.

Harriet is the author of several books, including Doing *Business with Ease Overseas: Building Cross-Cultural Relationships That Last*, which was selected for inclusion in the U.S. Library of Congress.

For more about this please visit www.harrietrussell.com/

Japanese Wisdom for Leadership

Quick Reference

腹芸

Haragei — The Art of the Belly

- Non-verbal, intuitive communication.
- Listening with your whole presence — silence, timing, and energy.
- Leadership lesson: Trust your gut. Influence is carried as much in presence as in words.

根回し

Nemawashi — Preparing the Roots

- The quiet groundwork of consensus-building.
- Conversations, alignment, and trust before public decisions.
- Leadership lesson: Do your inner and outer preparation before acting. Strong roots grow strong results.

甘え

Amae — The Courage to Lean

- Healthy dependence on others' benevolence. It is a gift to others when you allow them to help even if you don't "need" it.
- Recognizes our shared need for care and connection.
- Leadership lesson: True maturity includes knowing when to ask for help, and allowing interdependence to strengthen the team.

Our next chapter takes us out of theory and straight into the real world — where leadership is tested early, often, and without applause.

Introducing Kim Liddell, Australia

In Underground, **Kim Liddell** shares what it means to build credibility when you start with none. Not through titles, permission, or perfect conditions — but by showing up, doing the work, and carrying responsibility when it's heavy.

This is leadership learned at 6:30 a.m. on construction sites, in moments of being underestimated, in decisions that affect people's safety, livelihoods, and futures. It's about confidence that isn't claimed, but earned — underground, in the dark, one careful step at a time.

Kim reminds us that some of the most important leadership work happens where no one is watching, and that what we build beneath the surface is what holds everything up when pressure hits.

CHAPTER TWO

Underground

*Built confidence from the
ground up.*

One Careful Step at a Time

The site foreman crossed his arms when I pulled up. Six thirty in the morning, Western Sydney, Australia. The air already tasted like diesel and dust. I was there to quote on exposing a 150mm gas main before they could start digging footings for a new project. He looked at my truck, then at me, then past me, like maybe the real contractor was still coming.

"You the boss or the admin?"

I'd heard variations of this for six months straight. Sometimes they asked for "the guy who runs it." Sometimes they just waited, expectant, as if I were about to hand them a clipboard and point them toward someone else. I was thirty-four with a six-month-old baby and two sons, four and six, at home, and I'd just convinced the bank to extend our line of credit so I could buy a second vacuum excavation truck. The business was called Non Destructive Excavations Australia. The name made it sound like we had a fleet and a head office. I had one truck, a team of two, a mobile phone that rang at all hours, and me.

"I'm the one who'll dig it," I said. "You want to show me the drawings?"

He didn't move for a beat. Then he shrugged and walked me over to the plans spread across the tray of his truck. The gas main ran diagonally under where they needed to build. They'd already struck a services pit two days earlier with a backhoe and lost a day while everyone pointed fingers and wrote incident reports. He needed this done fast and right, but he didn't want to need me.

I took the job. I did the work. I invoiced on time. Six weeks later, his project manager called me for the next site.

That's how credibility gets built when you start with none. One job. One site. One foreman who doesn't trust you until, nothing's on fire, and the gas main was exactly where you said it would be, intact, exposed, ready for inspection. You do it again. And again. And eventually, the phone rings because they want you, not because they're stuck.

But I'm getting ahead of myself.

I didn't set out to build a construction company.

When I was five, I used to pack a little bag and tell my mum I was off to see the world. "Are you coming?" She was always too busy.

At twenty, I left Adelaide, South Australia, to sail on the STS Young Endeavour, a tall ship, for the coveted Passage Two of the World Voyage from Greece to America. I stayed in North America for two years after that, then kept moving. Four years in the Whitsunday Islands, off the coast of Queensland, Australia. Four in the Torres Strait, between Australia and Papua New Guinea. I wasn't running from anything. I was just allergic to staying still, to the idea that my life had to look like everyone else's life — steady job, mortgage, five-year plan. I worked where the work was interesting. I moved when the wind changed.

I landed in Sydney in 2003, and for the first time in my adult life, I stopped moving. Not because I'd changed, but because I saw something nobody else seemed to see.

Vacuum excavation. Non-destructive digging. Precision work in an industry built on brute force. Below the very ground we walk on is a vast and intricate city of infrastructure — optical fiber, gas mains, electrical conduits, water pipes, a web of buried utilities that keeps the lights on and the water running. All of it is invisible until someone with a backhoe puts a tooth through a 300mm water main and floods a street. Vacuum trucks use high-pressure water to break up soil and a vacuum system to remove it. No blades. No teeth. No catastrophic strikes. In Sydney in the early 2000s, almost no one was doing it. But the market was pulling hard. Contractors needed it. They just didn't know where to find it.

I bought my first truck in 2005 with a loan I wasn't sure I could service. The truck went to work the week I had my third child. I'd spent fifteen years moving. Now I was going to see what I could build if I stayed.

I ran the business from home years before the pandemic hit and working from home became commonplace. My life consisted of phone calls during nap time, quotes at the kitchen table after the kids were in bed, and coordinating crews while learning how to survive on four hours of sleep with a newborn. The first year, I learned that nobody cares about your business plan when a water main breaks at 2 a.m. They care if you answer the phone. They care if you show up. They care if you can find the pipe in the dark without taking out three other services in the process. I learned that a diesel engine doesn't care if you're tired or if your toddler had a nightmare or if you're trying to figure out how to pay two crews when one client hasn't paid you yet.

By the time my daughter was six months old, I'd recovered from a malignant melanoma diagnosis, and I started going back to sites for quotes and quality checks. That's when I learned the other cost of doing business as a woman in construction. Being underestimated has a compounding cost. Every site, every meeting, every quote… I had to prove I knew what I was doing before anyone would listen to what I actually knew. The "credibility tax," I called it. It's the invisible surcharge women pay just to be taken seriously in rooms full of men who assume competence until proven otherwise, while as women, we must prove it first.

Some days, I paid it without thinking. Some days, it made me so angry I had to sit in the truck for five minutes before I walked back onto the site.

Four years in, I had six trucks and twelve people on the books. The work kept coming, but so did the pressure. A contractor called me one Friday afternoon. They'd hit a fiber-optic cable with an auger during piling work for a new project in the inner west. The electricity rep was on site, the project manager was losing his mind, and they needed someone to expose the rest of the run before Monday or the whole job would stall. My crew was already committed to two other sites. I told him I'd be there in an hour.

My team spent that weekend on site, working 12-hour shifts to vacuum out meters of trench in clay that was half rock. Backs ached. Hands were blistered through gloves. By Sunday night, we had located and exposed all the services to enable safe construction work. I took a photo and emailed it to the project manager at 11 p.m. He called me Monday morning to thank me and book us for the next three phases.

That job paid well. It also cost me something I didn't notice until later. I'd stopped sleeping more than five hours a night. I'd started checking my phone before I got out of bed, during dinner, in the middle of conversations with my kids. I didn't talk about this with anyone. Not my husband, as he was dealing with his own challenges and inner struggles. Not my extended family. Not even my friends, because most of them didn't work in construction and wouldn't understand the rollercoaster of challenges.

But I did talk about it in my EO forum.

Questions and Answers

The Entrepreneurs' Organization (EO) was the first place I'd been in a room with people who understood that building a business means carrying a weight no one else can see. We met once a month — eight business owners from completely different industries, bound by a single rule: you could say anything in that room, and it stayed in that room. No advice. No judgement. Just presence and honesty, and the kind of questions that land sideways and make you realize you've been fooling yourself.

I told them I was tired. I didn't know how to step back without the whole thing collapsing. I was good at solving problems, but I wasn't building a company that could run without me.

One of the guys, who ran a logistics business, looked at me and said, "What if you did it differently?"

I didn't have an answer.

But the question stayed with me. And slowly, over the next year, I started testing it. I hired a contracts manager who was better at paperwork than I'd ever be. I trained two of my operators to run jobs without me checking in every three hours. I stopped answering my phone after 8 p.m. unless it was a genuine emergency, and I had to redefine what "emergency" actually meant because, in my head, everything felt urgent.

The business didn't collapse. In fact, it got stronger. We took on bigger clients. We won a contract to support a major rail corridor upgrade that lasted three years and became the foundation for everything that followed. I started getting calls from other contractors asking if we could train their people on non-destructive methods. We became the standard, not just a supplier.

But the cost didn't disappear. It just shifted. I'd built a reputation for being the person who showed up, who delivered, who didn't drop the ball. That reputation became its own kind of pressure. I couldn't just be good. I had to be flawless. Because one mistake — one missed call, one delayed response, one job that went sideways — would confirm what I knew some people were thinking: that I didn't really belong here.

Changing the Status Quo

I chaired Women in Civil from 2017 to 2024, a volunteer role that started as a single meeting and grew into a movement. When I started, women made up four percent of the civil construction workforce in New South Wales. Four percent. And seventy-six percent of those were in admin roles, not operating machinery or running sites. I wanted to change that, not with slogans or policy papers, but by showing up, making space, and proving that it could be done.

We launched the "50 by 50" campaign — 50 percent women in civil construction by 2050. Ambitious, maybe impossible, but it gave us something to aim at. We mentored. We profiled women who were already out there leading crews, running equipment, managing projects. We pushed for better amenities on sites, because if you don't have a toilet that locks or a crib room where you can eat lunch without being harassed, you're not staying.

The numbers moved. Slowly. By the time I stepped down, we were at nine percent. Still terrible, still a long way to go, but better than four. And the women who came through those programs —

who took those jobs, who stuck it out through the credibility tax and the casual sexism and the sheer physical grind — they're the ones changing the industry now, one site at a time.

I learned something from that work that applies to every kind of leadership. You can't wait for permission to make change. You can't wait for the conditions to be perfect or for everyone to agree that the problem is real. You just start. You show up. You do the work in front of you, and you bring people with you who are willing to move.

Sometimes, the work costs more than you planned to pay.

By 2020, I'd been running NDEA for fifteen years. We were the go-to contractor for vacuum excavation across Sydney. My kids were older. Jake and Brin were both competing in sailing at state and national levels, spending their weekends on the water the way I'd spent my twenties. Alexandra was in high school. The business was stable. I should have felt like I'd made it.

Instead, I felt like I was running on fumes.

Then the pandemic hit. Construction sites shut down, reopened, and shut down again. Contracts got delayed. Clients pulled back. Cash flow tightened. I spent hours on calls with suppliers, with banks, with clients, trying to keep everything moving.

And at the same time, I was Vice President of the Civil Contractors Federation of NSW, Chair of Women in Civil, President of my EO chapter, still showing up for my kids, still being the person everyone could rely on.

I started waking up at 4 a.m. and not being able to fall back asleep. I couldn't remember the last time I'd done something just because I wanted to, not just because it was on the schedule or someone needed me to handle it.

I didn't call it burnout. I called it a rough patch. I told myself I just needed to get through the next quarter, the next big job, the next board meeting. I told myself this was what leadership looked like —

holding it together when things got hard. But one night, sitting at the kitchen table with a spreadsheet open and a cold cup of tea I'd forgotten to drink, I realized I couldn't remember the last time I'd felt content with what I was doing. I felt competent. I felt capable. But contentment? Joy? The thing that had made me want to start this in the first place — the ability to raise my family on my own terms plus the satisfaction of seeing what I'd built — I couldn't find that passion anymore.

That was the moment I knew something had to change.

It took another three years to get there. Those years were spent restructuring, pulling back from day-to-day operations, and letting go of clients who didn't value the work we did. I learned how to lead from a place of intention, not just reaction. I accepted that I couldn't be everything to everyone — and that trying to be was making me smaller, not stronger.

I sold NDEA in October 2023. Eighteen years from the first truck to the final settlement, two weeks shy of my daughter's eighteenth birthday — my unusual twins coming of age together. It wasn't a dramatic exit or a huge payout, but it was clean and it was mine. I walked away from the business knowing it would keep running, that the people I'd trained would keep doing the work, and that the reputation we'd built was solid.

The five-year-old who packed her bag to see the world had finally stopped moving long enough to build something that would outlast her. Not because I'd changed. Because I'd learned that staying put doesn't mean staying small. It means going deep instead of wide. It means building infrastructure that holds, even when you're not the one holding it together.

And I walked away knowing something I couldn't have articulated when I started: that real confidence isn't about never doubting yourself. It's about doing the work anyway. It's about showing up to the site where no one thinks you belong and proving them wrong, not with words but with consistency. It's about building something that lasts, even when it costs more than you thought you had to give.

The credibility I earned didn't come from a title, a degree, or a big announcement. It came from eighteen years of showing up at 6:30 a.m. to sites where I had to prove myself every single time — until I didn't. It came from answering the phone at 2 a.m., solving the problem, getting the invoices out on time, and making payroll every week. It came from making the hard calls and living with the consequences, rather than looking to someone else to validate the decision.

That's what I call *Built Confidence*^{TM}. Earned through repetition, one job at a time, until you stop asking for permission and start trusting yourself.

Legacy Building

I still get calls from former clients. Some of them want to hire me for consulting work on large infrastructure projects. Some of them just want to catch up, to tell me about a job that went well or a problem they solved using a method I taught them years ago. And every time, I think about that foreman on that first site, the one who looked past me to see if the real contractor was still coming.

I wonder if he remembers me. Probably not. But I remember him, because he taught me that being underestimated is only a problem if you let it stop you. Every time someone doubted I could do the work, I had a choice. I could waste energy trying to convince them, or I could just do the work and let the results speak.

I chose the work. Every time. For eighteen years.

And now, when I stand on a construction site, walk into a boardroom, or sit across from someone trying to build something hard in a place where they don't quite fit, I lead with presence. I lead with the knowledge that confidence is something you build, underground, in the dark, one careful step at a time until you hit solid ground.

The city beneath the city. The infrastructure no one sees until something breaks. That's where you learn if you can hold the line when it matters.

And that's where you build something that lasts.

Reflection Questions

Where are you still trying to prove yourself instead of trusting what you've already earned?

What are you building that will outlast your presence?

— *Kim*

About Kim

Kim Liddell is a speaker, workshop leader, and former civil construction CEO whose leadership was forged under real pressure—where mistakes were expensive, credibility was earned, and results mattered. She didn't learn leadership from textbooks; she learned it in the dirt.

Raised without privilege, Kim developed grit, resourcefulness, and an instinct for problem-solving that became the foundation of her career. After identifying a gap in the market for safer excavation methods, she built a business from scratch—launching her first truck while raising young children and navigating serious personal health challenges.

Over the next decade, Kim scaled that single truck into a multi-million-dollar operation with more than 20 staff. She coined the term Non-Destructive Excavation, now an industry standard, served on national industry boards, co-founded initiatives supporting women in civil construction, and earned recognition for her contribution to the sector. Known as "Honest Kim," she became the operator clients trusted when failure was not an option.

After selling her company, Kim turned her focus to leadership from the inside out. Through her Optimised Living Framework, she helps people build real confidence, resilience, and sustainable performance. Her work is direct, grounded, and deeply human—designed for leaders who want clarity, capability, and longevity, not burnout.

For more information about Kim please visit
www.kimliddell.com.au/

Our next chapter invites us into one of the most defining questions of leadership:

What do you do when the right choice isn't the easy one?

Introducing Sarah Morse, Australia

In *The Courage Equation*, **Sarah Morse** reframes courage not as a heroic moment, but as a discipline built through small decisions, grounded purpose, and consistent action over time.
This chapter introduces a practical framework that shows how courage matures — from simply doing what is required, to creating long-term, systemic impact. Drawing on real-world experience from humanitarian work, healthcare, and leadership practice, Sarah demonstrates how values, transparency, and accountability shape cultures that protect people, not just policies.

This is a chapter about moving beyond minimum standards and into meaningful leadership — choosing what is right over what is easy, even when no one is watching.

CHAPTER THREE

The Courage Equation

Courage Begins in Small Places

I can still remember the cold green tiles and the smell of the old gas heater in our Year 12 Extension Math classroom. My textbook lay open, dense with symbols I couldn't decipher. Around me, the rest of the class worked with quiet confidence from years of physics and advanced science that I didn't have. I scribbled a question mark in the margin and slid my textbook toward Belinda, my equally bewildered friend, who responded with a helpless grin. We laughed, but underneath the humor was a familiar knot of fear. The fear of failure.

I knew how to study, how to perform, how to appear capable. But Extension Math was different. Velocity. Acceleration. Trajectory. Words that meant nothing to me and offered no clues to how to approach the problems. These equations did not bend to any amount of charm, extra effort, or hopeful guesswork.

After yet another disappointing test result, I slid into the car beside my mum and declared my decision to drop back to Basic Level Math. It felt like a responsible choice to retreat to solid ground where I knew I could excel.

Mum listened. Then she said words that would shape my leadership more than any school lesson: "You've always chosen things that come easily. Maybe it's time to choose something that's hard and expands your mind beyond what you think you can do. What if it's not about the mark you get, but who you become in the process?"

At seventeen, I didn't fully appreciate the wisdom, but I chose to stay with Extension Math. Mum found me a tutor, and I began to wrestle with concepts and equations that made me feel stupid. I learned to sit with frustration instead of fleeing from it. I tried to silence the voice in my head insisting I wasn't smart enough. I tried again.

I don't remember my final mark — only that it wasn't a disaster. But the mark wasn't the point. The point was the quiet courage I learned by staying with something hard: to persist without certainty and to endure discomfort without retreating. Courage began for me not in big decisions, but in the quiet, stubborn persistence of staying with a problem that felt too big for me to tackle on my own. It didn't feel heroic. It felt humbling.

Years later, I would learn that courage rarely arrives with fanfare. It begins as a whisper, a problem we can't ignore. For some of us, the problem is thrust upon us; others of us choose it. Courage isn't confidence — it's commitment.

This realization didn't happen overnight. It unfolded slowly over decades, across continents and careers, in hospital wards and remote communities, in boardrooms and safe houses. I learned that when courage is paired with purpose and multiplied by action, something extraordinary happens… We create impact.

Courage + Purpose × Action = Impact

This equation has become a framework I teach for leaders to move from intention to transformation.

The Courage Continuum

Before exploring the elements of the Courage Equation, it's important to understand how courage matures over time. Drawing from decades of work across humanitarian contexts, clinical practice, leadership, and modern slavery advocacy, I developed what I call the **Courage Continuum**. The Courage Continuum outlines the five stages leaders move through as they shift from compliance to transformational impact.

1. **Compliance Courage**

   Doing the minimum because a law, policy, or external pressure demands it. Necessary, but not transformative. It means we comply because we must.

2. **Conviction Courage**

   Acting based on personal or organizational values — even when no one is watching. We do it because it matters.

3. **Connection Courage**

   Understanding the human cost behind decisions and allowing compassion to guide responsibility. Recognizing that every number has a name.

4. **Systemic Courage**

   Challenging the structures that enable harm, and embedding ethics into operations, governance, and culture. Moving from individual responsibility to organizational transformation.

5. **Enduring Courage**

   Building long-term, measurable change that outlives your tenure and shapes future generations. Building systems, cultures, and commitments that protect people long after you're gone. It says: *We lead for those we may never meet.*

Every leader sits somewhere on this continuum. And the work of leadership — real leadership — is to keep moving forward and growing in courage.

Courage Beyond Compliance

Courage is often misunderstood as a dramatic, heroic force. But most courage is quiet. It whispers long before it roars. It invites us to take a step without knowing the outcome. It asks us to move without the safety of certainty.

In today's Environmental, Social and Governance (ESG) landscape, courage is not optional. It is a fundamental leadership capability. For too long, sustainability has been someone else's problem. The reality is that ESG leadership doesn't belong to sustainability experts alone.

Compliance is essential, but compliance alone will never dismantle harm. Compliance is the floor, the baseline we stand on. Courage is how leaders rise above it. It turns risk from something to manage into an opportunity to lead.

Courage shifts organizations from:

"What must we do?" to "What is the right thing to do?"

"How do we avoid risk?" to "How do we take responsibility?"

"How do we protect ourselves?" to "How do we protect others?"

Every leader has their version of that Year 12 math classroom — a moment when they realize they are standing at a crossroads, where they can retreat to safety and ignore the problem, or stay with the uncomfortable lessons and grow through hard things.

In ESG leadership, courage looks like:

- naming risks others prefer to ignore
- speaking honestly about supply chain vulnerabilities
- addressing harmful cultural patterns
- telling the truth before it becomes a headline
- choosing justice over convenience
- taking one step beyond the boundaries of certainty.

Courage begins the journey, but it is purpose that sustains it.

Conviction Courage – The Role of Purpose

The same year that I learned courage in a math classroom, I discovered my purpose in Africa.

After organizing the 40 Hour Famine fundraiser at school, I boldly cold-called local businessman and well-known philanthropist Dick Smith to ask if he'd match our fundraising efforts. Our school's $10,000 doubled to $20,000. That unexpected success led to an invitation to join a World Vision study tour in Zimbabwe and Zambia.

For the first time, I came face to face with the lived realities of poverty. Children greeted us with bright songs and generous smiles, but behind their joy were bodies marked by malnutrition. In schools where feeding programs operated, the meal they received at lunchtime was often the only substantial food they would eat that day. Hunger was no longer an abstract idea or a photograph in a brochure.

I met children who carried water for kilometers, mothers who rationed portions between their children, farmers who had lost their crops to drought, elderly grandparents raising their young grandchildren. Poverty was no longer a statistic. Behind every number was a name and a story. I smelled it, I felt it, I touched it.

That ten-day trip changed the trajectory of my life. I returned home devastated and awakened. With no qualifications, no grand plan, and no expertise, I understood something essential: awareness creates responsibility.

Once I had seen suffering, I could no longer pretend I hadn't. I couldn't unsee the things I had seen. I couldn't unknow them.

Purpose had taken root in my life's journey.

Over the years, purpose became the compass that guided me into cancer nursing, humanitarian and development work, and eventually, leadership. I learned that justice is slow, dignity is fragile, and that life does not deal the same portion evenly.

Purpose was no longer an idea. It was a direction.

Connected Courage

Purpose drew me into leadership, but it also exposed the limits of leading on conviction alone. I discovered that the leaders most driven by purpose are often the first to burn out — not because their purpose is flawed, but because their capacity is finite. They give at a rate their systems can't sustain. That's the tipping point: purpose without boundaries can become burnout; courage without rest can become recklessness; and impact without shared responsibility becomes unsustainable.

These imbalances don't just affect the individual; they shape the organization.

Purpose becomes meaningful only when it informs decisions, sets priorities, and defines the parameters that protect people and performance. It becomes a discipline that aligns culture with accountability, and the force that moves ESG from aspiration to implementation. When purpose is lived with boundaries and clarity, it doesn't just inspire leaders. It strengthens the systems that scale impact responsibly.

Purpose asks the questions that anchor responsible leadership:

- Who is affected by this decision?
- What do we have the power to influence?
- What does integrity require here?
- How can we improve our impact?

Purpose gives meaning to metrics and connects governance to humanity. It measures success not only by what we create, but by what we safeguard. It matures courage. It shifts leaders from compliance to conviction, and from conviction to connection. But purpose cannot work in isolation. To generate real impact, it must be paired with actions, boundaries, and systems that translate intention into accountability and change.

Systemic Courage Requires Action

I learned the power of purpose, as well as its limits, while working in a safe house for survivors of human trafficking in Spain.

By the time I was in my late thirties, I had been a cancer nurse and a clinical leader. I had decades of experience working in a Romanian orphanage, an African clinic, and communities struggling under the weight of poverty and displacement. But nothing prepared me for the weight of the stories held by the women who arrived at that safe house. Trauma layered on trauma. Exploitation so calculated it nearly broke me.

One bitter winter's morning, I was so exhausted, the cold seemed to penetrate my soul. Desperately grasping for anything to keep myself afloat, I paused at the bus stop on my way to work to buy a meditation coloring book and pencils — a small act of self-preservation.

As I arrived at the safe house, I met a Nigerian woman named Joy, who had arrived the night before. Shoulders hunched, hands clasped tightly, eyes distant, she shared fragments of her story, which were hauntingly familiar: denied education, caring for younger siblings, promised an opportunity to work abroad, trafficked, and forced into prostitution.

I asked softly whether there was anything I could get her that might help her settle in. She hesitated, then said shyly that at the temporary shelter she'd just left, she had found coloring in calming. "It helps me forget," she whispered.

Straight away, I reached into my bag and handed her the new coloring book and pencils.

Her eyes met mine and filled with tears. "How did you know?"

I didn't know. But a greater purpose propelled me that day.

A small act. Not a solution. Not a rescue. But a moment of human dignity.

That exchange didn't undo her trauma, but it changed the dynamic between us — two women standing at the intersection of compassion and connection, each using what was available in that moment. That's where connection courage starts, but to create greater impact, it requires action.

Working at the safe house and meeting women like Joy changed me.

For the thousandth time in my career, the gap between individual compassion and systemic injustice glared in front of me. Only this time, it snapped into sharp focus.

I realized that compassion and connection are essential types of courage, but compassion alone cannot dismantle exploitation. Connection courage sees the person, not the problem; systemic courage changes the systems that harmed them in the first place. Systemic problems need systemic change.

Action: The Multiplier

In leadership, especially in the ESG landscape, action is rarely glamorous. It is detailed, disciplined, and often invisible. It takes the sum of courage and purpose and multiplies it through action to create systemic impact.

Systemic courage looks like:

- mapping the real impact of decisions
- challenging systems that enable exploitation
- bringing transparency to uncomfortable truths
- ensuring policies translate into practice
- creating cultures where people can raise concerns safely.

Action is integrity — the alignment between what we say we value and what we consistently do. If you don't know where to start, start small. Start with what's in your hand and within your power to do. But don't *stay* small.

- Small actions reveal values.
- Repeated values create culture.
- Culture shapes systems.
- And systems scale impact.

Sprouts the seed

Becomes a seedling

Grows into a tree

Generates a forest!

In ESG-aligned leadership, credibility is built in moments far smaller than most leaders realize. The questions you ask in a meeting, the behaviors you reward, the risks you refuse to ignore — these micro-actions signal your organization's real values long before any report or framework does. When those values are demonstrated consistently, they don't just influence culture; they *become* the culture, setting the tone for ethical decision-making and responsible growth. That culture then shapes the systems you build: the policies that prevent harm, the governance structures that ensure transparency, and the processes that protect people throughout your operations and supply chain. Strong systems don't just maintain compliance — they amplify impact. They make responsible practice scalable, repeatable, and resilient. In this way, ESG performance isn't a project or just a report; it's a leadership choice repeated until it becomes the backbone of the organization.

Enduring Courage Creates Impact

After Spain, a new clarity emerged: if I wanted to support survivors of modern slavery, I needed to work with the systems that enable it to prevent exploitation before it occurs.

Modern slavery is not only a humanitarian issue. It is a leadership issue. A governance issue. A procurement and supply chain issue. A business issue. Every organization leaves an impact on people and planet. The question is: what kind of impact will it leave?

This question led my husband Stephen and me to establish Unchained Solutions — equipping organizations to lead beyond ESG compliance and unlock systemic impact. We equip leaders to understand that *ethical* leadership is not an optional extra, but a core part of organizational integrity, where courage, purpose, and action can be applied at a systemic scale.

Impact is the culmination of courage and purpose multiplied by action. It is powered by accountability. Impact measurement deepens courage because it asks leaders the hardest questions:

- How do we know what we do works?
- Who benefits?
- Who is harmed?
- What changes over time?
- What does "good" look like in practice?

Measurement is not the enemy of courage. It is the evidence of it.

I have repeatedly seen that when organizations begin measuring impact:

- Courage increases.
- Responsibility expands.
- Progress becomes visible.
- Teams recognize the influence they hold.

Impact invites leaders to step into Enduring Courage — the courage to build systems, safeguards, and cultures that outlive them. Impact is courage and purpose multiplied by action.

Enduring Courage asks:
- What are we responsible for?
- What scope is our sphere of influence?
- How will people experience the consequences of our decisions?
- How do we ensure impact survives leadership turnover?

Enduring Courage is a choice — a choice to build something that extends beyond individual leadership and shapes the future for those we may never meet.

Where the Equation Leads

As I reflect on my own leadership journey, I return to that Year 12 math classroom, and to having the courage to stay when the problem was bigger than me. I return as well to the villages in Zimbabwe and Zambia, where purpose first took root, and the safe house in Spain, where a small act of dignity highlighted the necessity of systemic change.

None of these moments were glamorous, but each one was formative. Each one pushed me further along the Courage Continuum. Each one revealed something essential about the Courage Equation:

- Courage starts the story.
- Purpose gives it meaning.
- Action makes it real.
- Impact is the legacy it leaves behind.

Leadership is the practice of bringing all four components together — imperfectly, consistently, courageously.

Not every leader will walk through famine-affected villages or survivor safe houses, but every leader will face moments that test their courage and encounter difficult problems that are bigger than themselves. Every leader will encounter decisions that affect human dignity. Every leader will find themselves at a crossroads where they will be asked:

Will you do what is easy — or what is right?

---

*"Courage is not the absence of fear. It is the
recognition that something matters more than fear."*
Franklin D. Roosevelt

When we choose courage beyond compliance, we don't just unlock processes; we unlock people. We don't just manage risk; we multiply dignity. We don't just protect brands; we protect lives.

The Courage Equation asks every leader: What would happen if your leadership aligned courage with purpose and expressed it through consistent, values-driven action?

What would change in your world if you led with courage — not just when it's expected, but when it's needed; not just when it's legal, but when it's right; not just when you're applauded, but when you're alone?

The answer is always the same: impact — the kind that strengthens trust, protects dignity, disrupts injustice, and creates a legacy.

Impact begins quietly. It grows in the moments no one sees. It is shaped in the choices we make under pressure. And it is built day by day through leaders willing to keep showing up — leaders committed to living their purpose and generating meaningful impact.

Leadership is the ongoing, courageous practice of shaping that legacy.

— Sarah

About Sarah

Sarah Morse has three decades of experience in humanitarian work, healthcare and leadership. As Founder, Director and Chief Storyteller of Unchained Solutions, she equips organizations to lead beyond compliance and unlock systemic impact.

Drawing on her work addressing modern slavery and supporting vulnerable communities, Sarah's keynote Unchained Courage and her chapter The Courage Equation inspire individuals to act with clarity, compassion, and conviction. She is committed to taking leaders on a journey of courage to live their purpose and make an impact. Sarah has received many awards for her service including NSW Young Australian of the Year and Women's Economic Forum Woman of Excellence.

For more information about Sarah please visit https://unchainedsolutions.com.au/keynote-and-facilitation/

Our next chapter brings us to the place where leadership actually happens — not in plans or policies, but in conversations.

Introducing Dr. Suresh Verghis, MCC, C-IQ, India

In *Mastering Conversational Agility*, **Suresh Verghis** reminds us that culture is shaped one conversation at a time. Trust, clarity, alignment, and momentum don't emerge by accident — they are created through how leaders listen, respond, pause, and speak under pressure.

This chapter explores the inner awareness required to lead well in dialogue and the practical skills that turn resistance into possibility, noise into focus, and tension into progress. Drawing on real leadership situations, Suresh shows how agile conversations build trust, surface truth, and enable better decisions when stakes are high.

Because when leadership conversations change, everything else follows.

CHAPTER FOUR

Mastering Conversational Agility

The Trust Primer: Setting the Tone Before You Speak

Conversations begin in the mind long before anyone says "Good morning." Leaders who understand this treat the opening moments of a dialogue the way architects treat foundations: everything that follows depends on how sturdy that base feels. Trust is the concrete. When team members believe their voice is valued and their dignity protected, they offer unfiltered insights, surface hidden risks, and accelerate innovation. Without trust, even brilliant ideas arrive wrapped in skepticism, and potential goes to waste. The trust primer is the deliberate, repeatable routine that signals safety and inclusion from the very first second.

Example: Before launching a contentious budget review, Jane, the operations head, moves the chairs into a circle, shares pastries, and opens by saying, "Our goal is to protect both margins and morale. Every viewpoint helps us do that. Let's agree that all challenges are directed at issues, never at people." The mood softens; analysts who usually demur begin asking bold questions, and the meeting ends with a joint savings plan everyone champions.

Practical exercise: In your next meeting, adopt a three-step trust primer.

First, state the positive purpose: why this conversation matters.

Second, invite participation explicitly: ask each person to name one outcome they're hoping for.

Third, establish a respect norm; for instance, "We will critique ideas, not individuals." After the meeting, reflect for five minutes on shifts in openness, tone, and the speed of decision-making.

Trust priming is less about grand gestures and more about consistent micro-signals. Eye contact, a focused agenda, and starting on time demonstrate reliability; laughter shows humanity; summarizing someone's point before responding shows care. Over time, these cues create an invisible safety net that allows teams to walk creative tightropes without fear of falling. Remember: you cannot retrofit trust after conflict erupts; you must pour the foundation early, cure it with presence, and reinforce it by acknowledging uncertainty honestly.

Saying "I may not have every answer, but together we will find a path" invites partnership instead of compliance and turns listeners into co-builders of success.

Choose that. Intentionally. Today.

Beyond First Reactions: Developing Inner Awareness

Self-awareness is the control tower of conversational agility, monitoring emotional weather and directing flights of thought so they avoid collisions. When leaders speak without noticing their internal state, turbulence ensues: sarcasm slips out, listening shuts down, and relationships bruise. Developing inner awareness means learning to detect physiological cues — tight shoulders, rapid breathing, clenched jaw — that precede unhelpful reactions. Noticing creates micro-seconds of choice where a different pathway can be selected, turning a potential flare-up into a chance for connection.

Example: During a quarterly review, Raj hears the CFO question the viability of his project. His pulse spikes, and the urge to defend flares. Instead, Raj inhales slowly, labels his sensation ("I'm feeling threatened"), and mentally asks, "What is the constructive intention behind her question?" He replies, "I hear concern about return on investment. Let me walk through the cost-benefit assumptions." The discussion remains analytical rather than adversarial, and the proposal survives with refinements.

Practical exercise: For one week, practice the STOP technique whenever tension arises:

S — Stop and notice physical sensations.

T — Take a slow breath.

O — Observe the story your mind is telling ("They're attacking me").

P — Proceed with a question that turns judgment into curiosity ("Help me understand your perspective").

Keep a pocket notebook and log each instance, rating how effectively you shifted from reflex to reflection.

Inner awareness is not self-absorption; it is self-management in service of connection. By naming emotions without acting them out, leaders model psychological maturity and grant others permission to reveal feelings safely. Teams led by aware managers report lower stress because unpredictable emotional outbursts disappear. Over time, this steadiness cultivates a climate where tough truths are voiced early, preventing costly surprises.

Developing awareness requires deliberate rituals. Morning check-ins, where you ask yourself, "What three emotions am I carrying into today?" build vocabulary. Mindful micro-breaks between meetings reset the nervous system. Scheduled Reflection Fridays invite pattern recognition: Which triggers repeat, and which responses produce the best outcomes? Remember, the goal is not emotional suppression but intelligent direction. It's like channeling electricity through insulated wires to light a room rather than spark a fire. Leaders who master their inner landscape find external landscapes less daunting because internal clarity breeds external composure. Practice daily, and you'll transform conversations.

Reframing Conversations: Turning Resistance into Possibility

Resistance is rarely pure opposition; it is protective energy guarding something people value. Agile leaders decode that energy and translate it into collaborative momentum by reframing the conversation. Reframing shifts the lens from problems to possibility, from blame to aspiration. It is the verbal equivalent of rotating a kaleidoscope: the same pieces form a new, more productive pattern.

Example: A product manager says, "Switching platforms will double our workload."

The innovation lead reframes: "I hear we care about manageable workloads. What if the new platform automates tasks and frees time for strategic projects?" Instantly, the discussion pivots from *burden* to *benefit*, opening room for creative planning.

Practical exercise: Identify a conversation where someone recently pushed back. Write their statement verbatim in the left column of a page. In the right column, list three possible values the statement might mask (e.g., stability, autonomy, excellence). Craft a response that acknowledges one value and offers a future-oriented option, starting with "What if…" or "How might we…" Deliver it in your next interaction.

The art of reframing relies on curiosity and imagination. Curiosity asks, "What positive intent could be hidden here?" Imagination tests alternative storylines until one ignites shared alignment.

Over time, habitual reframing rewires a team's collective narrative from scarcity ("We don't have enough resources") to resourcefulness ("How can we creatively deploy what we have?"). This mindset difference fuels innovation cultures where constraints become catalysts.

The language you use matters: swapping "but" for "and" invites expansion; replacing "have to" with "get to" encourages ownership. Even nonverbal framing, such as standing side by side at a whiteboard instead of across a table, signals partnership. Remember, the goal is not spin; it is surfacing overlooked angles that honor everyone's concerns while mobilizing forward energy.

Leaders skilled at reframing become organizational catalysts. They transform defensiveness into dialogue, complaints into design criteria, and conflicting agendas into complementary strengths. When people experience their perspectives being respectfully recast, fear loosens its grip and co-creation becomes possible. Each successful reframe strengthens trust and proves that alternative stories can drive superior results.

Refocusing Attention: Moving from Noise to What Matters

Complex conversations produce abundant data: opinions, emotions, facts, digressions. Without a method to prioritize, teams drown in noise and lose sight of purpose. Refocusing is the deliberate act of guiding attention back to the signal, to the shared intent that gives the conversation meaning. It is less about control and more about stewardship of collective cognitive energy.

Example: During a design sprint, engineers debate font sizes while the deadline looms. The facilitator intervenes: "Let's zoom out. Our sprint goal is a working prototype customers can test tomorrow. Font tweaks can wait; functionality cannot." The team agrees, redirects their effort, and meets the deadline.

Practical exercise: Before your next meeting, write the primary objective on a visible card. Whenever discussion drifts, raise the card silently or paraphrase: "How does this relate to our objective?" Track how often you need to intervene. Debrief by asking participants what helped them stay aligned.

Refocusing requires both noticing drift and having the courage to call it out. Signs of drift include rising volume around minor details, circular arguments, and side jokes that mask discomfort. A neutral, brief refocusing phrase anchors purpose: "Can we connect this point to our key outcome?" Overuse of authority suppresses creativity, while consistent references to purpose preserve autonomy within clear boundaries.

Digital tools help amplify a more refocused approach. Shared agendas with time-boxing, virtual whiteboards with goals highlighted, and countdown timers (Pomodoro technique) keep groups conscious of where attention belongs. Equally important are breaks: a five-minute pause can reset fatigued brains, making refocusing easier afterward.

Drama diminishes when purpose dominates. When people know why their conversation exists and how success will be measured, they self-correct their diversions. Leaders then become gardeners, pruning branches to let sunlight reach central growth. In a world saturated with information, disciplined focus is a strategic advantage that multiplies productivity, accelerates decision-making, and preserves the mental bandwidth teams need for breakthrough thinking.

Practice consistently.

Redirection with Intention: Steering Conversations Back on Track

Even well-framed, well-focused conversations can wander into unproductive territory: blame cycles, off-topic storytelling, or analysis paralysis. Redirection is the skill of steering the dialogue back toward constructive movement without diminishing contributors or glossing over real concerns. It involves acknowledging the current path, articulating a more helpful route, and inviting the group to agree to shift course.

Blame tells us where the pain is, but solutions tell us where the power is.

Example: In a cross-department stand-up, Marketing blames Operations for late data, Operations blames IT for system glitches, and tension rises. The project leader says, "I hear valid frustrations. Let's list one action each group can take this week to move forward." The energy pivots from finger-pointing to collaborative problem-solving.

Practical exercise: During your next meeting, listen for statements focused on past fault. When you hear one, paraphrase the concern, then pose a future-oriented question starting with "What would help us…?" or "How might we…?" Track whether the conversation shifts from history to possibility.

Effective redirection respects the reality of emotions. Simply suppressing negativity will breed resentment. Instead, name the emotion ("I sense frustration") and transition to agency ("What part of this is within our control today?"). This validates feelings while re-anchoring responsibility.

Timing is crucial. If you redirect too early, participants feel unheard; if you redirect too late, momentum stalls. A useful signal is repetitive looping — when the same point resurfaces without new information. That is the moment to pivot. "Let's shift gears" or "Can we park this for now?" provide clear direction. Visual "parking-lot" boards reassure contributors that their issues are noted for later.

Practiced regularly, redirection transforms culture. Psychological safety rises because people know missteps will be addressed constructively, not punitively. Over time, participants internalize the practice and self-redirect, freeing leaders to focus on vision instead of traffic control. Such autonomously constructive dialogue is the hallmark of a mature, high-performing organization.

Strategic Silence: The Power of Pause

Silence is not the absence of sound; it is the oxygen for thought. When words pause, the brain's threat circuits quieten and its insight networks light up, turning discomfort into discovery. Conversationally agile leaders employ silence as a precision tool — to let emotions settle, to invite unheard voices, and to emphasize pivotal ideas.

They know that a deliberate pause can land harder than the most eloquent speech.

Example: Quarterly results arrive well below forecast. The sales director feels the team bracing for blame. Instead of reacting, she closes her laptop, folds her hands, and looks around the table without speaking. After 20 seconds, a junior analyst breaks the hush: "We relied too heavily on one segment. I have a diversification plan." The silence converts fear into ownership and initiates solution-focused dialogue.

Practical exercise: Before your next meeting, choose two moments — after presenting data and after asking a question — where you will hold a 10-second pause. Time yourself discreetly. Observe who contributes, what quality of insight emerges, and how the room's energy shifts.

Debrief privately: Did the pause feel longer than it was? What new information surfaced?

To master strategic silence, pay attention to your body language. Maintain soft eye contact, relaxed shoulders, and an encouraging nod so the pause feels invitational, not punitive. Pair silence with acknowledgement — "I'm letting that sit for a moment" — to normalize reflection. Use the technique sparingly; overuse dulls its edge.

Silence also serves as a reset button during heated exchanges. If voices escalate, the leader can say, "Let's take 30 silent seconds to gather our thoughts," then model slow breathing. Physiologically, this lowers cortisol and steadies heart rates, restoring a collaborative climate.

Finally, integrate micro-silences into daily conversation. After someone speaks, count "one-and-two" before responding; the gap demonstrates respect and often elicits additional nuance. Cumulatively, such pocket pauses cultivate a culture where reflection precedes reaction and insight outranks impulse. In a noisy world, silence remains the most underleveraged leadership resource. It is free, renewable, and astonishingly powerful when wielded with intention. Remember: people seldom recall every sentence you utter, but they always remember how a meaningful silence made them think, feel, and step forward.

Reading the Room: Listening Beyond Words

Conversations happen on at least three channels: verbal content, vocal tone, and visual cues. Reading the room means tuning all antennas, decoding the unspoken, and adjusting course before misalignment hardens into resistance. Leaders skilled in this art perceive not only what is said but also sighs, side glances, and the collective pulse. They position themselves as real-time diagnosticians, continuously asking, "Where is the energy now, and what does it need?"

Example: During a merger briefing, the CEO notices folded arms and foot tapping from the legacy company's managers. Rather than continue the slide deck, she pauses and says, "I sense concern about how roles may change. Let's surface those worries." By naming the emotional undercurrent, she legitimizes feelings, invites candor, and reduces hallway speculation.

Practical exercise: For one week, practice the Three Lenses scan in every meeting.

Lens One – Eyes: observe posture shifts and facial expressions.

Lens Two – Ears: track vocal pace, volume, and hesitations.

Lens Three – Intuition: register gut impressions of the atmosphere.

After the meeting, journal your observations and any adaptive actions you took. Patterns will sharpen perception and agility.

Reading the room requires genuine curiosity; people detect insincere analysis. Approach cues as data, not as judgments. If someone crosses their arms, ask yourself, "Could that signal cold, fatigue, or dissent?" Check assumptions aloud: "I might be misreading, but I'm sensing hesitation. What's on your mind?" This invitational stance converts observation into dialogue.

Environmental factors matter. Dim lighting, seating arrangements, or virtual lag may distort signals. Adjust the context: open blinds, rearrange chairs, or build in camera-off minutes to create clearer feedback loops. For remote teams, leverage polls, reaction emojis, and breakout chats to surface sentiment.

Advanced readers watch group dynamics like a weather map: storms of disagreement, high-pressure silence, warm currents of enthusiasm. They deploy matching interventions — probing questions, energizing stories, or concise summaries. Mastery emerges when adaptation feels seamless, participants feel seen, and progress accelerates without explicit commands.

Co-Shaping Meaning: Tools for Shared Understanding

Exchange becomes transformation when people move from telling and selling to co-shaping meaning. Shared meaning emerges through externalization — putting ideas out where everyone can see, question, and refine them — and through iterative synthesis, the process of connecting fragments into a coherent whole. Leaders who facilitate this process use visual tools, plain language, and structured reflection to convert scattered insights into collective intelligence.

Example: A cross-functional team wrestles with conflicting customer feedback. The facilitator opens a digital whiteboard and asks each member to post one sticky note per observed pain point. In silence, 40 notes appear. The group then clusters themes, labels patterns, and agrees on three root causes. What began as cacophony turns into an aligned improvement roadmap — created by all, owned by all.

Practical exercise: During your next planning session, introduce a "build-on board." Invite participants to write ideas or questions on cards and place them publicly. The rule: every new card must link to, expand, or challenge an existing card. After 20 minutes, review clusters and draft a one-sentence summary for each. This visual lineage reveals how thoughts evolve together.

At the outset, define key terms such as "customer success," "minimum viable," or "risk," and revisit definitions when confusion arises. Misaligned semantics are responsible for many silent derailments. Early alignment prevents wasted cycles.

Whether using sticky notes or sophisticated collaboration platforms, the leader's stance should be "Let's explore possibilities" rather than "Let's decide fast." Paradoxically, taking time to generate and integrate perspectives often shortens total project duration because rework shrinks.

Watch for dominance patterns. If two voices frame all clusters, intentionally invite quieter members to contribute: "Joyce, what do you see that's missing?" Psychological safety broadens the data pool and enriches conclusions.

End sessions with synthesis rituals. Ask, "What story are we telling now that we weren't telling an hour ago?" Capture the group narrative in shared documents so momentum continues post-meeting. Collective authorship begets collective ownership — and that drives execution with lasting impact.

The Agility Mindset: Leading Conversations that Create Change

Techniques matter, but mindset determines whether they are applied transactionally or transformationally. The agility mindset treats every dialogue as a living laboratory for learning, adaptation, and co-creation. Leaders who hold this mindset combine clear intent with flexible pathways. They orient to purpose, stay curious about emerging data, and pivot quickly without ego when reality suggests a better route.

Example: A manufacturing VP launches a weekly "learning huddle," where frontline operators, engineers, and managers bring micro-problems to solve in 30 minutes. The rules: no blaming, quick experiments, and shared learnings posted company-wide. Within three months, defect rates drop 15 percent and employee suggestions triple. The VP's mindset of iterative discovery turns routine meetings into an engine of continuous improvement.

Practical exercise: Choose a recurring meeting you lead. Draft a one-sentence purpose that emphasizes exploration and growth. For example: "We gather to surface insights and test small actions that move us closer to our goal." Share this at the next session and invite participants to propose a single experiment for the coming week. At the subsequent meeting, review results, capture lessons, and select the next experiment. Track momentum over four cycles.

Cultivating the agility mindset involves three daily micro-practices. First, begin mornings by asking, "What am I eager to learn today?" Second, during conversations, replace at least one statement with an open question that starts "What if…?" or "How might…?" Third, end the day with a two-minute reflection: "Where did I adapt well? Where did I cling to certainty?" Small loops drive big growth.

Constant change without direction breeds chaos. Anchor flexibility to North Star values and measurable outcomes. When people understand why shifts occur, they ride the waves willingly rather than brace against them.

Organizations led by agility-minded leaders exhibit faster innovation cycles, higher engagement, and greater resilience during disruption. Teams internalize the message: experiments are safe, feedback is fuel, and failure is data. Over time, conversational agility becomes cultural agility — embedded norms that extend beyond any single leader and keep the enterprise vibrant, responsive, future-ready, and able to seize opportunities before competitors even perceive them.

— Suresh

About Suresh

Dr. Suresh Verghis is a global keynote speaker, executive leadership coach, author, and facilitator with over three decades of experience helping leaders grow with clarity, courage, and purpose. He is the Founder Director of Global Coach Resources LLP and serves as visiting faculty at leading institutions, including the Indian Institutes of Management and the Great Lakes Institute of Management, Chennai.

His professional journey includes senior HR leadership roles with AB Mauri, Associated British Foods PLC, and Heidelberger Druckmaschinen AG India, where he led complex people and organizational development initiatives across cultures and geographies. These experiences shape his grounded, practical approach to leadership and transformation.

At the core of Suresh's work is a belief that meaningful leadership begins with inner work. He is the author of *Money on Meaning*, a book that reflects his conviction that lasting success comes from aligning performance with purpose. With over 8,000 hours of executive coaching and learning interventions delivered to more than 50,000 professionals, his expertise spans Emotional Intelligence, Personal Effectiveness, High-Performance Teams, Change Leadership, and Conversational Intelligence.

Suresh is an ICF Master Certified Coach® and Certified Mentor Coach. In recognition of his contribution to leadership development, he was awarded a Doctorate in Management (Honoris Causa) in 2020 by the George Washington University of Peace, Florida, USA.

For more information about Suresh please find him on Linkedin: www.linkedin.com/in/sureshverghis

References

Glaser, J. E. (2013). Conversational intelligence: How great leaders build trust and get extraordinary results. Bibliomotion.

Goleman, D. (1995). Emotional intelligence: Why it can matter more than IQ. Bantam Books.

Schein, E. H. (2013). Humble inquiry: The gentle art of asking instead of telling. Berrett-Koehler.

Rosenberg, M. B. (2003). Nonviolent communication: A language of life. PuddleDancer Press.

Edmondson, A. C. (2019). The fearless organization: Creating psychological safety in the workplace for learning, innovation, and growth. Wiley.

Covey, S. R. (1989). The 7 habits of highly effective people. Simon & Schuster.

Scott, S. (2002). Fierce conversations: Achieving success at work and in life, one conversation at a time. Berkley Publishing.

Patterson, K., Grenny, J., McMillan, R., & Switzler, A. (2002). Crucial conversations: Tools for talking when stakes are high. McGraw-Hill.

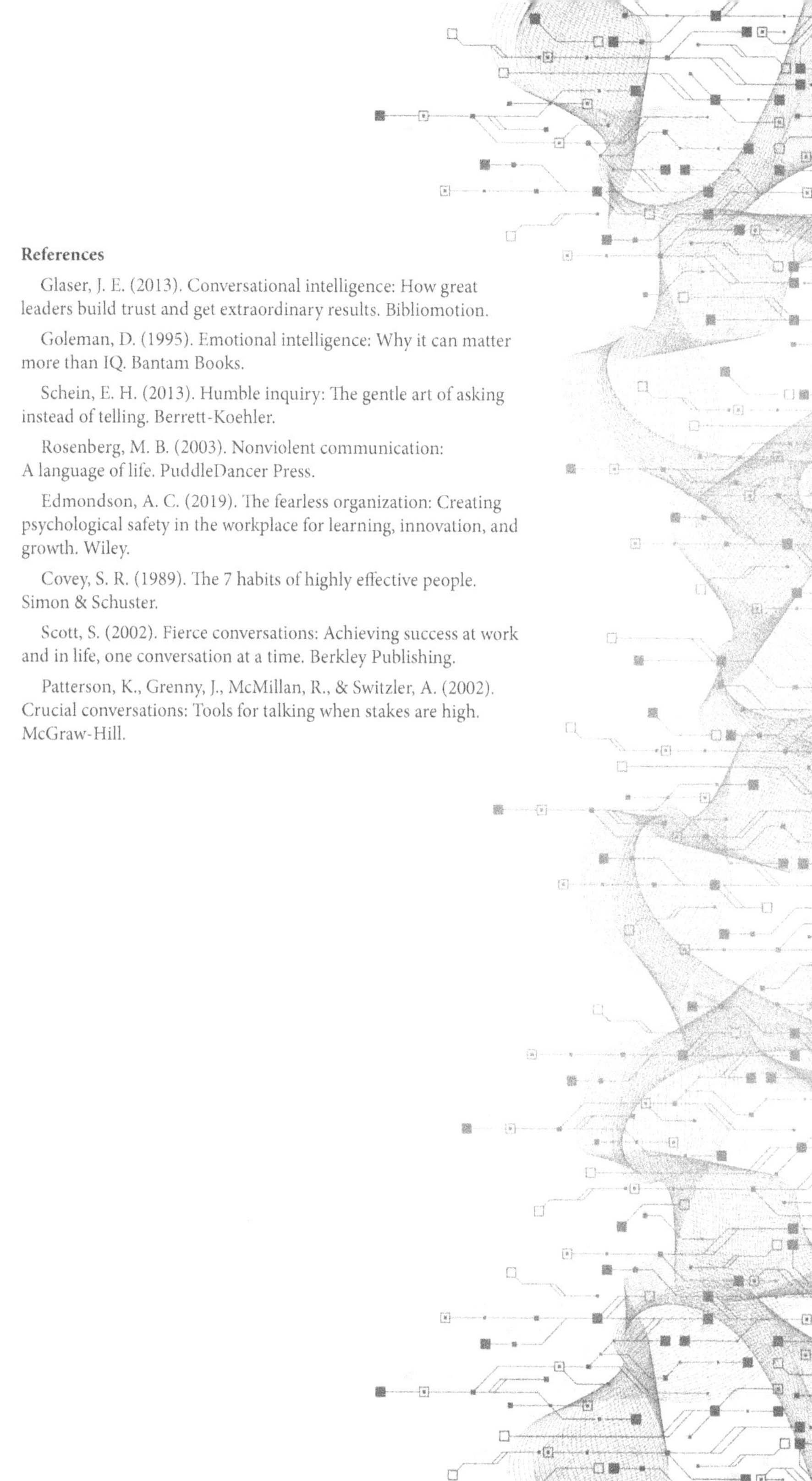

Our next chapter steps into a space most leaders try to avoid — but shouldn't.

Friction.

Introducing Claudia Cimenti, Luxembourg

In *Leading Through Friction*, **Claudia Cimenti** reframes tension, conflict, and discomfort not as problems to eliminate, but as signals to work with. Because in leadership, friction is often where growth begins.

This chapter explores the inner game of leadership — what happens inside us when pressure rises, perspectives clash, and decisions matter. Claudia shows how leaders who learn to stay present in friction can transform uncertainty into clarity, self-doubt into confidence, and conflict into forward momentum.

Rather than smoothing things over or pushing through, this chapter invites leaders to engage tension intelligently — and to discover how the right kind of friction can become a powerful source of innovation and competitive advantage.

CHAPTER FIVE

Leading Through Friction

Leveraging Team Tension for Growth

You know that moment when the air shifts in a room? The conversation drops off mid-sentence. People are suddenly fascinated with their phones. Someone clears their throat and suggests, "Maybe we should table this for now."

Your chest feels tight. The meeting started with such promising energy, but suddenly it feels like a bomb is about to go off. Everyone is wondering: How can we leave without making things worse?

What if I told you, however, that those moments are invitations rather than warning signs? What if the obstacle that makes you want to run is actually a powerful catalyst for success?

My years of coaching executives through their messiest challenges have shown me a consistent pattern. Leaders who learn to work with healthy tension, not against it, don't just survive conflict; they transform it into their competitive edge. The teams that built real innovation, trust, and resilience? They did it by harnessing friction, not avoiding it.

Even Einstein liked to quote the anonymous proverb: "In the middle of difficulty lies opportunity." When you handle conflict skillfully, it becomes the forge for shared understanding, better decisions, and the kind of deep buy-in you only get through real participation. Let me show you this through a story that captures what I see again and again — a composite drawn from dozens of leaders who've walked into the same storm and discovered something they never expected.

A Story of Tension

Janet was riding high when she got promoted to vice president. Her fintech company had just acquired a promising startup, and she was tasked with integrating the teams. Her own people, "the originals," were scrappy and fast. They'd built the company on gut instinct, quick pivots, and whatever-it-takes energy. The acquired team? Brilliant analysts who lived for data, process, and methodical planning.

This will be exciting, Janet thought. *Those skill sets complement each other and will certainly make for one unstoppable team.*

The first meetings held promise. Everyone was polite, eager, and professional. But around week three, things shifted. Conversations became arduous. The originals would pitch an idea, and the new team would respond with, "We should probably run some numbers on that." Eye rolls. Barely concealed sighs. Then someone would suggest, "Let's park that for now," and the room would deflate.

Janet found herself playing referee. "Marcus, tell us more about the risk analysis," she'd say, then quickly add, "And Lisa, I love that you're thinking big picture." But her diplomatic dance wasn't working. Progress slowed to a crawl. Deadlines started sliding. The energy that once drove both teams was fading fast.

Her CEO noticed. "Janet," he said during their one-on-one, his voice carrying an edge she hadn't heard before, "I'm not seeing that magic we talked about. What's happening over there?"

Janet's stomach dropped. She knew exactly what was happening, but she didn't know how to fix it. So she did what felt safest: she separated the teams. Let the analysts work on their models in peace. Let the originals run their rapid experiments. Shorter meetings. Less friction. Problem solved, right?

Wrong.

The company actually started moving backward. A major product launch was pushed back for the third time because nobody could agree on priorities. A star engineer quit, citing "unclear decision-making." During one particularly brutal video call, two team leads argued for 20 minutes about whose timeline mattered more, then spent the next three weeks communicating only via passive-aggressive email.

Janet was lying awake at 3 a.m., replaying conversations, wondering where she'd lost control. The team that was supposed to be the company's secret weapon was becoming its biggest liability.

Then came the meeting that changed everything.

Janet walked into the conference room, looked around at the carefully neutral faces, and made a decision that quietly terrified her. She closed her laptop, took a breath, and said, "Okay, I need to say something. We're failing. Not because anyone here isn't smart or committed, but because we're all pretending everything's fine when it obviously isn't."

The silence was deafening. Janet's heart was pounding, but she pushed through. "So right now, in this room, I want to know: What's really in the way? No politics, no diplomacy. Just the truth."

For what felt like forever, nobody spoke. Janet could hear the air conditioning, the distant sound of traffic. Her palms were sweating. Then Marcus, one of the quieter analysts, cleared his throat.

"Honestly? Half the time I have no idea who's actually supposed to make decisions. We spend hours debating stuff, and then someone from the other side just goes ahead and does whatever they were going to do anyway."

Lisa from the original team leaned forward. "And we feel like every idea gets buried in analysis paralysis. By the time you guys finish studying something, the opportunity's gone."

Something cracked open in that room. Not pretty, not comfortable, but real. One by one they started talking. About feeling dismissed. About confusion over roles. About loving their work but hating the dysfunction.

Janet didn't try to fix anything. She just listened, asked questions, let the mess be messy. By the end of that two-hour session, something had shifted. People weren't just venting; they were proposing solutions, volunteering for different roles, even laughing about their mutual frustrations.

Three weeks later, they shipped their pilot project on schedule for the first time in months. As Janet reflected later, "We didn't solve all our problems in that meeting. But we finally started talking productively about the real issues. Once we stopped pretending, we could actually move."

Why Friction Is Your Hidden Asset

I could share many stories like Janet's. Most leaders I work with believe that conflict equals failure and should be avoided, managed, or eliminated at all costs. However, research shows that teams that understand conflict as a spark for creativity rather than a threat to performance are more likely to trust deeply, take meaningful risks, and innovate in ways that matter[1].

When you tell your team that friction is a sign of failure, you teach them to suppress their real worries. Surface harmony becomes more important than actual progress. But if you choose to make productive tension a part of how you work, you'll notice problems sooner, bring out points of view that would otherwise stay hidden, and keep learning alive when it matters most.

What is the real cost of avoiding friction? It's not just missed chances; it's also the gradual decline of engagement, the loss of your best talent, and, ultimately, the erosion of competitive ground your company may never reclaim.

The Four Faces of Team Friction

Here's the thing about friction: not all of it is the same. One of the fastest ways to turn manageable tension into organizational crisis is to treat every conflict as though it requires the same solution.

Let's further explore different types of conflict.

1. **Structural Friction**

This is the friction originating from unclear boundaries, overlapping responsibilities, and confusing decision-making processes. Janet's team hit this wall hard: talented people were stepping on each other's toes not because they couldn't work together, but because the system itself lacked clarity.

Don't you see this everywhere in growing companies? What worked when you had 30 people completely breaks down at 300. Large modern systems create friction points: cross-functional teams, matrix reporting, distributed leadership, teams of teams… Add remote work, multiple time zones, and digital collaboration platforms, and the complexity multiplies fast.

---

1   (Edmondson & Bransby, 2023).

The main point is that this systemic friction goes beyond personalities and communication styles. It's driven by hidden structural knots that even well-intentioned people get tangled in. Trying to solve it with team-building exercises will just frustrate everyone involved.

2. **Interpersonal Friction**

Every team has its mix of personalities: the high-energy extrovert, the thoughtful introvert, the person who thinks out loud, the one who needs time to process. But what looks like a personality clash is often something deeper — a fundamental difference in how people approach work, process information, or communicate.

It makes me think of the product manager who needs to talk through every decision and the engineer who wants detailed written specs before any discussion. Their conflicts aren't personal; they're rooted in completely different problem-solving systems.

In the virtual workplace, these differences get amplified. The person who's quiet on video calls might be your deepest thinker, but they can appear disengaged. The natural interrupter dominates even more when everyone's stuck in gallery view. Reading the room becomes exponentially harder when half the room is muted and off-camera.

3. **Cultural Friction**

Culture isn't just about nationality, though that's part of it. It's the invisible playbook every group develops — the unwritten rules about how work gets done, how feedback gets delivered, and how decisions get made.

I worked with a Luxembourg-based team where the French sales manager, American operations director, and Portuguese finance lead kept hitting walls. Not because they disagreed on the pillars of their strategy, but because their basic assumptions about everything from what "on time" means to how you signal disagreement were completely different.

Culture shapes what people say and what goes unsaid… which is exactly how misunderstandings and real conflict begin.

Cultural friction shows up between departments too. Engineering's "get it right before we ship" versus marketing's "iterate fast and learn." Sales' relationship-first approach versus finance's numbers-first mindset. Different generations, different work styles, different definitions of what quality and speed actually mean. *The challenge is real.*

Culture shapes what people say and what goes unsaid… which is exactly how misunderstandings and real conflict begin.

4. Cognitive Friction

This is the friction that emerges when smart people look at the same situation and see completely different realities — not because someone's wrong, but because they're working from different frameworks, priorities, or ways of understanding the problem.

I recall of a biotech company, where half the leadership team wanted to focus on their most promising existing drug and the other half wanted to diversify into new therapeutic areas. Both sides had compelling arguments, solid data, and reasonable concerns. They weren't stuck because they lacked information; they were stuck because they couldn't see that their different perspectives were actually the raw material for a better strategy.

The best teams let cognitive diversity breathe, then channel its tension into breakthrough insights. The worst teams try to force consensus — and lose half the value of having diverse thinkers in the room.

Why Recognition Beats Resolution

Almost every leader's first instinct when friction appears is to make it go away. Call a team meeting. Send everyone to communication training. Create a new process. Do something — anything — to get back to smooth sailing.

But here's what I've learned: if you don't correctly diagnose the type of friction you're facing, your well-intentioned solutions often make things worse. Team-building exercises can't fix structural confusion. Communication workshops won't resolve fundamental strategic disagreements.

The critical move is recognition: learning to "read" the friction accurately before you try to channel it. I call it Friction Typing[IP]. Like a skilled physician, the best leaders diagnose before they prescribe.

Take Maya, a director at a fast-growing software company. She kept investing in communication skills training for her team, but the real problem was that three different people believed they were responsible for the same decisions. All the active listening techniques in the world couldn't fix that structural mess.

When you're not sure what type of friction you're looking at, start by asking some diagnostic questions:

- Which tasks keep getting duplicated or falling through the cracks?
- Who says "that's not my call" most often, and why?
- Where do people debate for hours without ever reaching decisions, and what's really driving that?

You'll be surprised how quickly honest answers illuminate the real patterns. And remember: you don't have to figure this out alone. Your biggest resource for understanding team friction is the team itself. Get them involved in the diagnosis.

The Conflict Comfort Spectrum

Let's talk about you for a minute. When conflict shows up in your team, what's your instinctive response? Do you feel your shoulders tense as you start looking for ways to smooth things over? Or do you feel a little energized, like finally the real conversation can begin?

The conflict comfort spectrum goes from "harmony-seeking" (you want to avoid conflict, so you chase agreement and quick fixes) to "confrontation-comfortable" (you enjoy a healthy fight). Most leaders don't fit the extremes; they bounce around depending on the stakes, the players, and how much pressure is in the room. Understanding where you naturally land, and expanding your range, is crucial for leading through friction effectively.

"Harmony-seekers" typically keep things calm and moving. If not careful, however, they may accidentally foster false consensus, where team members never voice their real objections in order to appear agreeable. Problems get swept under the rug, only to show up downstream, multiplied.

Conflict Courage[IP] is not about enjoying conflict, nor reflexively shutting it down, nor letting it disrupt clarity and action. It's about channeling it productively.

"Confrontation-comfortable" leaders get energy from creative tension. Debate is oxygen to them. But without discipline, they can shut down quieter voices, intimidate others, or prompt surface-level agreement that masks deeper resistance.

The best leaders find what I call the sweet spot. They're comfortable with friction's first appearance, able to tolerate discomfort, and brave enough to call it out early. They exhibit what I call "Conflict Courage[IP]." It's not about loving conflict, nor reflexively shutting it down, nor letting it disrupt clarity and action. It's about channeling it productively.

I fondly remember my coaching client Fatima, a seasoned senior executive at a wealth management firm. Her team meetings had become all too polite, predictable, and completely devoid of energy. Everyone nodded, nobody challenged anything, and their strategies were getting stale.

Fatima told me that during one particularly lifeless session, she stopped mid-presentation, looked around the room, and asked, "Okay, who thinks this approach is wrong? And why haven't you said so?"

The silence that followed felt like an eternity. Fatima later told me her heart was racing as this wasn't her natural style at all. But she held the pause, and eventually, hesitant hands started going up.

Three Steps: From Friction to Growth

Let's get practical. When I study teams that consistently transform friction into forward momentum, The following three moves out of my Fertile Friction Framework[IP] make the difference.

Step 1 - Recognize: Develop Your Tension Radar

From my observations, the most valuable leadership skill you can develop is the ability to sense and type friction early, before it turns into deeper dysfunction. This requires curiously examining every interaction, every meeting, every Slack thread as data. Every watercooler conversation can be a source of information about your team's dynamic.

Here are examples of what to watch for:

- Changes in participation patterns (who's talking more, who's going quiet)

- Shifts in energy or pace (meetings that drag, conversations that stall)

- Nonverbal cues (eye rolls, sighs, people multitasking more than usual)

- Topics that get repeatedly postponed or "taken offline"

- Jokes or complaints that keep surfacing

And pay attention to your own reactions. Which people or subjects make you anxious? When do you find yourself talking faster or backing down? Your own discomfort is often the first signal that friction needs attention.

Try this exercise: Keep a "tension diary" for one week. After every meeting or team interaction, jot down one sentence about the energy you sensed. Were people engaged or just going through motions? Did certain topics create visible discomfort? Over seven days, you'll start seeing patterns you might have missed.

I remember working with a global retail company where the European team leader noticed people were having side conversations in WhatsApp during video calls. What looked like multitasking was actually three team members who had given up on voicing disagreement in the main conversation. Once she invited those WhatsApp threads into a safe, open space, trust increased overnight, and real issues finally got addressed.

Step 2 - Reframe: From Problem to Possibility

The language you use to describe friction shapes how your team responds to it. Label tension as a problem, and everyone goes into defensive mode. Frame it as useful information or creative energy, and you open up entirely different possibilities.

- Instead of saying "We have a conflict," try "We have different perspectives that might lead to a stronger solution."

- Instead of "There's tension between departments," try "We're discovering opportunities to align our priorities more effectively."
- Instead of "This is causing problems," try "This might be highlighting something important we need to address."

I worked with a consulting firm in Luxembourg where the leadership team was split on whether to expand internationally or strengthen their local market position. For months, meetings alternated between heated debate and icy silence. Everyone was frustrated.

The breakthrough came when their CEO stopped a particularly tense discussion and said, "Wait. What if this isn't a problem we need to solve, but information we need to use? Maybe our division of views means that we haven't fully explored yet what success looks like."

The room went quiet. Then someone said, "What if we mapped out what each approach is trying to protect or achieve?" Within two hours, they'd collectively designed a hybrid strategy that addressed everyone's core concerns. The heated debates became collaborative exploration.

Practice reframing in real time. When someone uses "problem" language about team friction, pause and ask, "What might this tension be trying to tell us?"

Step 3 - Recalibrate: Make Friction Work for You

Conflict-typing and reframing are just the first steps. Now friction needs to be channeled into forward movement. This requires creating structures and processes that make this conflict safe and generative.

Here's an example of what works:
- Ask better questions. Instead of "What's the right answer?"

try "What's each perspective trying to protect or achieve?" Instead of "Who's right?" ask "What would we need to believe for each approach to make sense?"

- Separate positions from interests. When people are arguing about budget allocations, dig into what those resources represent: security, growth, recognition, impact. When you understand the underlying interests, creative solutions become possible.

- Use time intentionally. Some friction needs space to unfold. Other conflicts benefit from time pressure. Learn to time-box difficult conversations: "Let's explore this tension for 20 minutes, then decide our next step."

- Create experiments. When teams are deadlocked, turn debate into data. "Let's test both approaches on a small scale and compare results in two weeks."

- Build in reflection. After working through any friction, always ask: "What helped? What made it harder? What would we do differently next time?" This is how teams get better at productive conflict.

A startup product manager once told me, "I realized I kept avoiding asking if people disagreed because I had no idea what I'd do if they said yes." That insight changed everything for her. She started routinely ending presentations with, "What concerns or different perspectives haven't we heard yet?" — and then actually made space for the answers.

I know of a financial services team that went so far as to create a new norm: every major decision had to be followed by at least one small experiment that tested different approaches. The quality of their choices improved dramatically over six months, and more importantly, over time people felt heard and engaged in ways they hadn't experienced before.

Living the Practice

None of this matters if it stays theoretical. Here's how to start building these capabilities right now:

- Self-assess honestly. Where do you fall on the conflict-comfort spectrum? If you tend to avoid tension, practice sitting with discomfort before rushing to solutions. If you're naturally confrontational, work on creating more psychological safety for others.

- Notice patterns without fixing them. For the next week, just observe. What makes energy spike or plummet in meetings? Which topics does your team consistently avoid? Don't intervene yet. Just build your own pattern recognition.

- Experiment with reframing. When you hear "problem" language about team dynamics, practice offering a possibility reframe: "Maybe this disagreement is showing us something important about our priorities."

- Start small. Pick one low-stakes conflict or tension point and try the Three-Step Process: *recognize* what type of friction you're dealing with, *reframe* it as information rather than threat, then create one small experiment to *recalibrate* it productively.

- Involve your team. Share some of these concepts and ask for their input: "How do we typically handle disagreement? What works well, and where could we improve?" Most teams are hungry for this kind of conversation.

Some detailed tools and templates for these practices will be available in bonus materials I've included access to at the end. But you can start making progress with just these foundational moves.

Take care of yourself in this work. Leading through friction doesn't mean loving every moment of discomfort; it means building the stamina and skill to see conflict as information, not threat.

An Invitation

Please consider my invitation to you... what if you shifted from leading *away from* conflict to leveraging it? What if you measured your leadership effectiveness less by how often meetings end nicely and quietly, and more by how consistently your team moves through struggle into clarity, action, and progress?

The question isn't whether you'll encounter friction, but rather whether you'll help your team transform it into the kind of growth and innovation that only comes from working through difficulty together.

Every organization, from a local SME to a multinational enterprise, has friction. Most teams, however, tend to ignore or minimize it. The exceptional ones? They get curious about it, creative with it, and ultimately turn it into competitive advantage. The tension is already in your team, your organization, and your industry. The question isn't whether you'll encounter friction, but whether you'll help your team transform it into the kind of growth and innovation that only comes from working through difficulty together. Step into that difficult conversation. Hold space for the uncomfortable pause. Let friction become your pathway to breakthrough.

— *Claudia*

About Claudia

Claudia Cimenti is an Executive Thinking Partner and leadership coach who helps leaders master the inner game of leadership — enabling executives, entrepreneurs, and teams to move from pressure and self-doubt to clarity, confidence, and bold decision-making.

Through her proprietary Fertile Friction Framework[IP], Claudia works with leaders and organizations to transform tension and conflict into catalysts for innovation, growth, and sustainable competitive advantage.

With roots in Luxembourg and extensive international experience, Claudia brings a rare and practical perspective on navigating the complexities of intercultural leadership. She supports leaders of global and diverse workforces to lead with presence, adaptability, and impact across cultural boundaries.

Claudia is EMCC-accredited as both a coach and team coach, a certified mediator and conflict resolution specialist, and a published author of leadership books. Based in Luxembourg and working virtually worldwide, she is fluent in English, Luxembourgish, German, and French — enabling authentic connection with diverse stakeholders across regions and industries.

For more information and bonus materials visit:
http://www.topcoach.lu/leading-through-friction

References

Chism, M. (2022). From conflict to courage. Berrett-Koehler Publishers.

Edmondson, A. C. (2019). The fearless organization: Creating psychological safety in the workplace for learning, innovation, and growth. Wiley.

Edmondson, A. C., & Bransby, D. P. (2023). Psychological safety comes of age: Observed themes in an established literature. Annual Review of Organizational Psychology and Organizational Behavior, 10, 55–78.

Folger, J. P., Poole, M. S., & Stutman, R. K. (2020). Working through conflict: Strategies for relationships, groups, and organizations. Routledge.

Hoover, J., & DiSilvestro, R. P. (2005). The art of constructive confrontation: How to achieve more accountability with less conflict. John Wiley & Sons.

Liddle, D. (2017). Managing conflict. Kogan Page.

Papke, E. (2015). The elephant in the boardroom: How leaders use and manage conflict to achieve greater levels of success. Career Press.

Runde, C. E., & Flanagan, T. A. (2008). Building conflict competent teams: The skills you need to handle conflict constructively. Jossey-Bass.

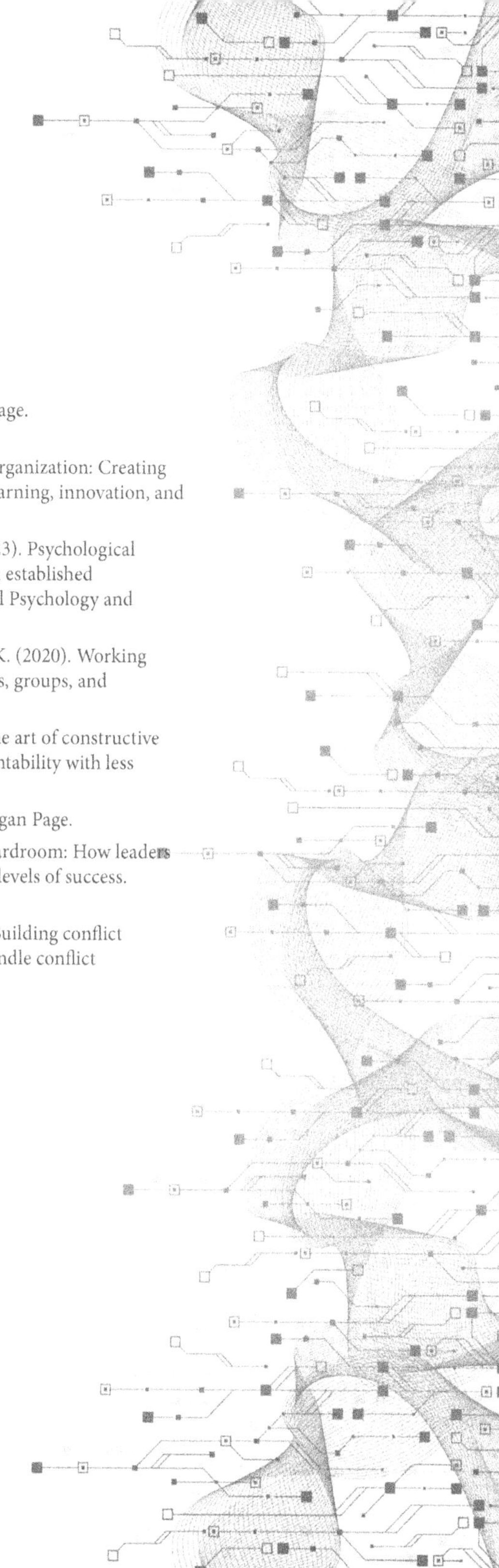

Our next session takes us into territory every leader faces — but too few truly own: risk.

Often misunderstood. Frequently outsourced. Sometimes ignored until it's too late.

Introducing Bronwyn Reid, Australia

In this chapter, **Bronwyn Reid** argues that effective leadership isn't about avoiding risk, nor about reckless bravado. It's about setting the tone, building a culture where risk is understood at every level, and knowing when to lean into opportunity — and when to protect against downside.

This is not a compliance conversation. It's a leadership one. Because, as Bronwyn reminds us, **risk is not the enemy of leadership — it is the proving ground.**

CHAPTER SIX

Leadership in a World of Risk

The 1980s: Confidence Without Caution

Vision of Leadership in the 1980s

I spent my formative years in business during the 1980s, an era of large shoulder pads, skyrocketing share markets, and strong-man leadership (yes, it was almost exclusively men). The prevailing leadership model was a mix of charisma, aggression, and the pursuit of profit. If you did not experience these times, do a quick search for these names: Alan Bond, Robert Holmes à Court, John Elliott, and Christopher Skase. These leaders didn't ask permission. They didn't ask questions. They barked orders and expected results. It was an aggressive, chest-beating style. And many of them, on the surface, "succeeded," at least for a short time. The economic winds were at their backs, and risk, if it was considered at all, was seen as something to be conquered, not managed.

The 1980s were a time of peak business optimism, and it felt as though anything was possible. There was money to be made, deals to be done, and no time for what was perceived as hand-wringing over "what-ifs."

- The Cold War was slowly drawing to a close.
- Massive financial reforms unleashed the Australian economy.
- Stock markets boomed.
- China's industrial production was growing at 20% per annum, and its GDP by 10% per annum.
- We were still living in the shadow of Milton Friedman's "The purpose of a corporation is to make a profit for its shareholders" doctrine, first published in 1970.

Somewhere through that decade, the concept of risk was put on the backburner. Everything was going to be permanently fine and dandy. "It's different this time" was a regular quote from the commentariat.

The Reckoning

It did not end well.

In Australia, the final reckoning came on October 20, 1987. After rising 381% over the preceding five years, the stock market fell 25% in one day. The risk-taking behaviors of corporate titans — excessive borrowing, poor oversight, weak boards, cronyism, inflated balance sheets, and short-termism — came back to bite them.

Companies that had been darlings of the market collapsed overnight. Investors lost fortunes. And the leaders who had never needed to think seriously about downside scenarios suddenly found themselves exposed.

Economist Michael Reddell summed it up:

Internal guidelines … were routinely ignored and redefined to suit, and recordkeeping and reporting systems were grossly inadequate. Auditors rarely asked hard questions (and had they done so, would no doubt have jeopardized their mandate), and no one any-where seems to have wanted to explore the possibility that things could go very badly wrong.[1]

Some went quickly, others slowly — but the fate of the high-flyers was inevitable. Bond Corporation, Bell Group, Rothwells, GPI Leisure, Tricontinental, Qintex, Adelaide Steamship... Many names disappeared, and some of the perpetrators went to prison.

Not an Outlier

The point of this story about the 1980s is twofold:

- It's a revelatory lesson in what happens when risk is ignored.
- It illustrates that we keep making the same mistake: ignoring risk.

The 1980s weren't unique. Unfortunately, the pattern has repeated:

- The Tech Boom and Bust (1995–2000)
- The Global Financial Crisis (2007–2008)
- The Australian Mining Boom and Bust (2003–2012)

And it will happen again. Whenever you hear "It's different this time," it's time to get your risk radar out, fine-tune it, and start paying attention. It seems that, in business, memories are always short. In the great Australian resources-industry bust of 2012–2013, I spoke to innumerable business owners who swore blind that next time they wouldn't fall for the hype and encouragement (and bullying) of the mining industry. Maybe they won't, but there will be a whole new crop of business owners ready to ignore the discipline of risk management.

It's not just booms and busts (as well as floods, fires, cyclones, heart attacks, divorces, sickness, accidents, new technology, legislative changes...) either. They are inevitable, and yet collectively and individually we never seem to be prepared.

---

1   https://croakingcassandra.com/2016/08/15/tricontinental-revisiting-the-financial-disasters-of-the-1980s/

What Risk Management Really Means

A better alternative is to have your risk radar permanently switched on.

Risk management isn't a bureaucratic exercise; it's a leadership mindset.

If you ask ten business owners to define "risk management," you'll get ten different answers. Some will stare blankly. Others might mention a spreadsheet or checkbox-filled register they used for a tender application — and never looked at again.

That's not risk management. That's paperwork. Risk management isn't a bureaucratic exercise; it's a leadership mindset.

At its core, risk management is simply:

1. Identifying what could go wrong
2. Thinking through what the consequences would be
3. Working out what you can do to stop it happening, or what you'll do if it does happen.

That's it. It's not complicated, but it *is* critical. Because here's the truth:

If you're not managing your risks, you're leaving your leadership to luck.

I've watched too many good businesses get blindsided, not because they were unethical or incompetent or careless, but because they didn't see changes coming. Or they thought, That doesn't apply to us. Or worse: We'll deal with that when it happens.

Unfortunately, risk management still has a branding problem. People think it's about fear, or lawyers, or ticking boxes. At least, that's how far too many business owners and managers treat it, often because they have no idea where to start.

I want to introduce you to an extraordinarily useful tool for examining risk. You've probably heard of it, but may

- not really know what it means, or
- not realize that it's an invaluable addition to your leadership skills.

Understanding ESG as a Risk Management Tool

You may have heard of these letters but passed them by as just another business acronym that doesn't apply to you. But it does, and it's not just another waste of time and money.

The letters stand for:

- **E**nvironmental – your impact on the environment
- **S**ocial – your impact on your community
- **G**overnance – how you make decisions and run your company.

Collectively, ESG is how we measure the performance of an organization beyond its simple financial achievements. We have been measuring financial performance for centuries, and we are now expanding to other critical aspects of business operations — ***environmental impact, social responsibility, and governance practices***.

It's a rather awkward acronym. The three letters simply stand for two adjectives and a noun, so I add an "R" at the end for Reporting, or Responsibilities. Both those words imply action — that you have to *do* something, either report on something or take responsibility for something. It will help you to understand the concept if you keep that silent 'R' in mind, as a reminder that ESG is something you have to *do*, not just a random concept that somebody thought up.

Two Frameworks = Double Impact

I have now introduced you to two frameworks:

- Risk Management

- Environmental, Social, and Governance (Responsibilities)

Unfortunately, both are underused and often unloved. Far too often, both are treated as "box-ticking" exercises, just another thing to fit into your already overloaded role description as a business owner or manager.

But the frameworks are not just about compliance. They're not checklists. They're a combined decision-making framework.

Here's the magic: When you combine ESG with risk thinking, they become your forward-facing radar, helping you see what's ahead and not just cover what's behind.

- You go from defensive to strategic.

- You stop reacting and start looking ahead.

ESG helps you see the broader impacts of your decisions:

- How will this affect our reputation?

- Are we exposed to climate, regulatory, or social shifts?

- Is our team culture strong enough to weather a storm?

ESG is risk management with depth. It invites you to look not just at what could hurt *you*, but what could hurt the environment, your stakeholders, your community, your license to operate.

These days, that's what leadership demands.

The corporate high-flyers (aka cowboys) of the 1980s were distinctly deficient in their use of both frameworks. (To be fair, the acronym ESG wasn't widely used then, but the elements of environmental, social, and governance responsibility certainly were.)

In the past, risk was often seen as something you could put in a neat little box: financial risk, operational risk, compliance risk. You created some operating policies, took out some insurance, and maybe a consultant helped you tick the right boxes. The unspoken assumption was that if you did those things, you had "managed" risk.

But real life doesn't work that way. Risks don't line up obediently into categories. They overlap, spill over, and combine in ways that consistently catch even well-prepared leaders by surprise. A natural disaster such as a big storm, flood, earthquake, or even an unexpected drought isn't just an environmental risk; it can quickly evolve into a financial crisis, a reputational headache, and a safety issue all at once. A regulatory change can turn into a supply chain disruption, which then becomes a staff retention problem. The COVID-19 pandemic was a perfect illustration of just how messy risk (and hence, risk management) can become.

For small businesses, this messy reality is amplified. Larger organizations often have the luxury of being able to absorb shocks. For a smaller company, those same events can seriously threaten survival. That, right there, is why leaders of a small to medium-sized business must be attuned towards risk management.

There are also risks that are hard to measure. Community trust, for example, is not something you can insure against, but when trust is lost, the damage can be immense. Trust takes years to build but can be lost in a single incident. There are ample examples of companies that have had their reputations shredded because they failed to listen to stakeholders or dismissed community concerns. Mining company Rio Tinto is a cautionary example.

In 2020, Rio Tinto, one of the world's largest companies, destroyed the 46,000-year-old Juukan Gorge caves in the Pilbara region of Western Australia. The site was of cultural and archaeological significance to the Traditional Owners of the area, the Kunti Kurrama and Pinikura (PKKP) peoples. Rio Tinto had ministerial consent under the prevailing laws but failed to consider the ethical and social implications. Legal approval does not equal social license, and the company paid a huge price for this action.

Their ultimate costs included:

- A media storm and global outrage
- The resignation (under pressure) of some executives
- Investor withdrawal — impacting severely on funding, causing job losses and broader instability
- A severely tainted reputation

A parliamentary inquiry resulted, and legislation was changed. The company's defense was that the action was legal. I'm certain that there was an exhaustive risk management process pertaining to the safety aspects of the operation (blowing up large amounts of dirt and rock is hazardous), but it obviously didn't go further than that. Had the decision-makers applied an ESG lens to their risk assessment of whether to go ahead, they would have avoided all the unwanted outcomes.

In summary, Rio Tinto illustrated that protecting your legal backside is not sufficient. They didn't consider responsibilities, relationships, trust, community license, investor confidence… Rio Tinto followed the law but failed in leadership, social responsibility, ethics, transparency, and governance.

You may be thinking: That's a giant company, not me and my small business. But even if your business is small, the lesson stands.

I clearly remember the cafe that put up the price of a coffee to $11 per cup during the floods we experienced in my own community in 2010–2011. Yes, I know all about supply and demand, but more than doubling the cost of a coffee didn't go down well. (A good coffee can do wonders in a physical-crisis situation.) Many locals took a long time to forget that, and some have never purchased anything from that café again.

The Nature of Risk in Modern Business
Risk Isn't New — But It's Evolving

Whenever someone says, "Business is riskier now than it used to be," I smile. I'm sure our predecessors thought the same. Imagine leading a business on the Australian or American frontier a century ago, with very little communication, transport, or healthcare. Or during the Industrial Revolution, when entire industries vanished overnight. Think of the earthquakes in Christchurch, New Zealand, or the Boxing Day tsunami in Indonesia.

Risk has always been the shadow side of opportunity. Of course, some risks are permanent and unchanging, but new ones emerge over time. Climate change is a clear example of a risk that wasn't talked about just decades ago.

One major change is how fast risk can spread. I mentioned the COVID-19 pandemic earlier, one that certainly wasn't on my risk radar, and it spread quickly. Globalization has intensified everything and added urgency to the already messy business of dealing with risk. Tariff changes in the United States affected Australian industries overnight, rapid advances in technology mean cybercriminals are on your digital doorstep, and a single post on social media can damage a brand in hours.

So What Does This Mean For Leaders?

Risk can't be treated as an afterthought the way it often was during the 1980s. It isn't just the compliance officer's job; it's a critical part of leadership itself. As a leader, you set the tone for how risks are identified, discussed, and managed. You create the culture that decides whether people speak up about a problem or sweep it under the rug.

I want to end on a positive note and encourage you not only to see the potential downside of risk but also to see the opportunities that risk management presents. The same uncertainty that creates risk also creates space for innovation and advantage. Leaders who understand this, and who can balance caution with courage, will be far better equipped to navigate their organizations to sustainable success.

If you want to delve deeper in to this, I invite you to download a complimentary copy of my latest book: ***Small Business Big Impact: Why ESG Won't Save You But Smart Strategy & Real Action Will.*** Follow the QR Code for details.

— Bronwyn

About Bronwyn

Bronwyn Reid is a business leader, author, and risk management practitioner with almost 30 years' experience and developed expertise in the regional business sector of Australia. She is co-founder and director of 4T Consultants, a multi-award winning environmental business working with major organizations and local communities, where safety, compliance, and sound decision-making matter every day. Bronwyn is also the author of *Small Company – Big Business; Small Company – Big Crisis; Small Company – Big Purpose;* and co-author of *Small Business – Big Impact.* She writes and speaks about leadership, risk, resilience, and ESG, with a focus on helping leaders stay steady under pressure and build businesses that earn trust over time.

If you want to find out more please visit: www.bronwynreid.com.au

Leadership, courage, conversations, risk, humanity, and technology all converge here — in influence.

Introducing Ravin Souvendra Papiah, Mauritius

In The Influence TRIAD, **Ravin Souvendra Papiah** explores how leaders translate intention into impact through the powerful intersection of leadership, communication, and trust.

This chapter focuses on how influence is built — not through authority or persuasion alone, but through clarity, credibility, and connection. Ravin shows how leaders who understand this triad can lead conversations, shape decisions, and move people ethically and effectively in complex environments.

As the closing chapter of the book, The Influence TRIAD leaves readers with a practical lens for applying everything they've learned — turning insight into action and leadership into lasting impact.

CHAPTER SEVEN

The Influence TRIAD

How I Built my Global Stage

Early Learnings

I learned to read an audience long before I ever stood behind a lectern. My first audience did not sit in rows; they bent beneath the sugarcane sun. In those fields, a pausing wind could feel like permission, and the hush of a tired mother could say more than any speech ever would. I didn't yet know the word "influence," but I knew what it meant to feel people before I spoke to them. I knew the discipline of listening and the power of presence without performance.

Years later, in a bank office with more forms than feelings, I watched numbers walk in dressed as people and discovered they carried stories. Targets mattered, but trust decided everything. Later still, I would lead across borders and learn a harsher wisdom: even when your vision is generous, people can be hurt by how you carry it. Titles don't protect you from the test of humility; they invite it. In those moments I began to see what my life had been assembling all along: the **Influence TRIAD — Public Speaking, Sales, and Leadership** — not as three disconnected skills, but as a single current running through the work of becoming useful to others.

Public speaking is how you **move hearts**.

Sales is how you **move decisions**.

Leadership is how you **move people and systems together**.

Master them in isolation, and you will achieve.

Weave them, and you will transform.

This is that weave.

Public Speaking – The Power to Move People

*Content without connection leaves a room respectful…
and unchanged.*

I did not begin on grand stages. I began by learning to stand inside myself. My first speeches were not speeches at all; they were attempts at courage. In early meetings, my voice carried words but not weight. I prepared diligently, but some part of me stayed backstage. The truth is this: content without connection leaves a room respectful… and unchanged.

The turning point came the day I allowed my real story into the microphone. Not the glossy résumé, but the raw ascent — the sugarcane beginnings, the first serious job at age 19, the seasons where money taught me how fragile certainty can be, the slow work of rebuilding, the decision to serve beyond my comfort. I stopped performing as a "speaker" and began showing up as Ravin. The energy in the room changed. Eyes lifted. I didn't become more polished; I became present.

Concept — Speaking is not performance; it is transfer.

A speech is a vehicle that moves belief from one heart to many. Slides don't move belief. Conviction does. Story does. A clear promise to the audience does. You are not there to impress them; you are there to upgrade their future in the time you are given.

So how do you build content and speaking that truly moves people?

You begin before you write. I stand at the threshold of every talk and ask the most important question in my craft: *What will be different for them because I came?* The answer becomes a single line — the spine of the speech. Not a theme. A promise. If I cannot name it, I am not ready to take their time.

Sales is not the art of pressure; it is the art of permission: helping someone say yes to the future they actually want.

Then I choose one story that only I can tell, from a life I have actually lived. The story is not decoration; it is the engine. I do not bring the story to flatter myself; I bring it because an honest story is a mirror that lets people recognize themselves. If a detail does not serve the promise, I cut it. If a paragraph flatters me but doesn't free them, I cut it. Mercy for the audience is the beginning of mastery.

I speak in pictures and in steps. Pictures help people feel; steps help them act. I slow down when the idea asks for respect. I allow the pause to do part of the work. I refuse to shout what a whisper can say better. Most of all, I keep the center clean. The talk is not about my brilliance; it is about their belonging — to a future, to a standard, to their own voice.

When the final sentence comes, I do not end with "Thank you" if "Let's begin" will serve them more. The goal is not clapping hands; it is moving feet.

Law of Public Speaking

Your message is not what you say; it is what they can now do. Speak so people move.

Sales — The Art of Influence with Integrity

Before I called it sales, I called it survival. I grew up in a world where every day required a trade — effort for food, time for school, courage for dignity. Later, sales became formal: the bank counters, the presentations, the proposals; and in my entrepreneurial journey where I eventually became a *Senior Eagle Manager* — a top-tier international leadership and sales achievement status in the Forever Living Products network marketing business. It became the discipline of turning value into livelihood — without losing your soul.

People misunderstand sales. They think it is talk, scripts, push. The best salespeople I know do more research than rhetoric, more listening than lines. The biggest wins in my life did not come because I convinced someone. They came because I understood someone — their pain, their hope, the cost of staying the same. Sales is not the art of pressure; it is the art of permission: helping someone say yes to the future they actually want.

I discovered this the hard way. In my early days, I mistook enthusiasm for service. I talked too soon. I offered solutions to problems that had not been named aloud. When I learned to qualify with kindness — to ask the humane questions, to measure timing and fit with respect — sales stopped feeling like a chase and started feeling like a collaboration. The close was no longer a wrestle; it was a relief.

Concept — Sales is ethical alignment

You are aligning three things: a real problem, a real solution, and a real decision. Anything less is noise. When those three align, momentum happens. When they don't, manipulation happens.

Here is how I work it now, and how I teach it:

I begin with discovery, not a demo. What is the felt problem beneath the presented problem? What is the emotional cost of the status quo? What is the time cost? What have they tried? What failed and why? I don't interrogate; I **witness**. The right questions make people wise about their own lives.

Then I reflect their world back to them cleanly — not to corner them, but to confirm we are seeing the same picture. I ask permission to offer a way forward. Only then do I present. And when I present, I do not drown them in features; I move from pain to path to proof:

- Here is the pain you named.
- Here is the path I propose.
- Here is the proof that it is possible (results, stories, data, references that are real).

I price with spine. If the value is there, the price is an act of honesty. If the value is not there, I do not discount; I rescope. I do not sell what they don't need; I sequence what they do. I follow up like a professional, not a beggar. The tone is never "please pick me." The tone is "here's the next clean step whenever you're ready."

And when a "no" comes, I practice graceful exit. There are many rooms in the house of timing. Doors that close today are opened later by people who were treated with respect.

Sales made me a better human because it forced me to replace the hunger to win with the hunger to understand. In the end, the goal is not a signed paper; it is a sustained relationship that justifies the signature.

Law of Sales

Sales is not getting people to agree with you; it is helping them agree with their best future.

Leadership – The Responsibility to Multiply Others

If speaking is how you move hearts and sales is how you move decisions, leadership is how you move a whole community forward without leaving its soul behind. It is the art of stewarding momentum *and* belonging at the same time. This is where the TRIAD matures: your words matter, your conversions matter — but your character is the container that either sustains or spills both.

I learned this in rooms where passion was high and pressure higher. Leading across nine nations — Angola, Eswatini, Mozambique, Mauritius, Madagascar, Malawi, Zambia, Zimbabwe, and South Africa — I have felt the beauty and complexity of building across borders and bandwidth. Culture speaks. History speaks. Fatigue speaks. And your own style, however efficient, can still cut where you intend to heal.

There was a season when the core leadership team I was working closely with felt hurt by my communication. They never questioned my dedication to the work we were jointly pursuing, but they wondered whether my urgency had begun to overshadow their dignity. I apologized, and although I believed I had been giving them everything I had, I still walked away with a heavy truth: impact is not intention. If the people you lead feel smaller around you, your results are an expensive illusion.

Leadership is not about being right for people. It is about being safe for people — safe enough that they can bring you the truth early. You cannot fix what you are not told. You will not be told if your presence costs too much.

Concept — Leadership is the compounding of courage and care.
Courage to name reality, to set a standard, to decide when others hesitate. Care to protect dignity, to build capacity, to repair quickly when you bruise what you meant to build. Strip either one out and you get distortion. Courage without care becomes cruelty; care without courage becomes chaos.

How do you practice it?

I manage energy before strategy. Teams don't move because a plan is clever; they move because a leader's calm conviction makes work feel doable. Before a high-stakes discussion, I settle my own weather. I enter rooms as a thermostat, not a thermometer — setting climate, not echoing heat.

I communicate standards without contempt. We will do world-class work — not because we chase perfection, but because the people we serve deserve our best. I attach standards to purpose, not to ego. I make "why" a habit, not a keynote.

I build systems that carry kindness: clear roles, clean meetings, short feedback loops, quick apologies. We celebrate courage, not just outcomes. We reward candor that prevents waste. We keep receipts of learning: what worked, what didn't, what we will do differently by Friday.

I protect time for thinking. Leaders confuse speed with stewardship. Pace is not progress if direction is wrong. Weekly "white space" is not a luxury; it is oxygen. In that space I revisit the three questions that keep me honest: *Who am I becoming while I build this? Who are they becoming with me? What will endure when we are gone?* Legacy is built in those answers.

Above all, I repair. Not performative apologies; real repair. For example, I do not apologize for having standards; I apologize for the way I carried them if I made people small. The *speed* of repair demonstrates the *sincerity* of leadership.

Leadership done this way transforms rooms. People do not merely work with you; they grow near you. You see them stand taller in their own lives. That is the only scoreboard that lasts.

Law of Leadership

Power is what you can do; leadership is what others can do because you came.

The Weave – How the Three Become One

The TRIAD is not three silos to master in sequence. It is one river with three currents. I have never given a great talk without doing real sales work beforehand — discovery, empathy, promise. I have never led well without speaking with clarity and selling a future worth sacrifice. I have never sold with integrity without the heart of leadership asking, *What does this decision make them become?*

When public speaking, sales, and leadership interlock, several quiet miracles happen:

- **Your message gains traction.** Public speaking shapes the narrative so people know what to feel and do next. Sales converts that movement into real commitments. Leadership sustains those commitments in systems that keep promises.

- **Your character becomes the brand.** Speaking showcases your conviction. Sales tests your alignment. Leadership proves your consistency. The market forgives mistakes; it does not forgive double standards.

- **Your presence multiplies.** As you move across these domains with the same spirit, people trust you faster. You spend less energy convincing and more energy **compounding**.

Think of it this way:

- Speaking without sales is *inspiration without adoption*.

- Sales without leadership is *transaction without transformation.*

- Leadership without speaking is *direction without devotion.*

The masterpiece is the weave.

Practicing the TRIAD Daily - Living the Influence Habit

Mastery is not built in conferences. It is forged in the ordinary rhythm of your days.

The Influence TRIAD is not something you switch on when you step onto a stage. It's something you practice quietly, between emails, meetings, and moments of reflection.

Here's how I invite you to live it with me, one ordinary day at a time…

Begin every important day with one promise sentence.

Who will be different because of you by evening? The clearer the promise, the cleaner your speaking, the kinder your sales, the braver your leadership.

Treat every conversation as discovery before delivery.

Whether you're pitching a program, presenting a budget, or setting a standard, ask two more questions than your impatience wants. People rise when they feel seen.

Use story like a doorway, not a mirror.

Your story is not to admire yourself; it is to invite them in. Share the piece that unlocks their courage, then get out of the way.

Price like a professional; serve like a priest.

Let numbers be honest and service be generous. If price is a struggle, adjust the scope, not your spine.

Hold silence until the right words arrive.

Presence grows when you stop needing to prove you deserve the room. Breathe. Choose words that carry *the people*, not *your ego*.

Apologize at the speed of truth.

Repair quickly when your tone outruns your care. Nothing compounds trust faster.

Leave every room with a next visible step.

Great speaking clarifies action. Great sales schedules action. Great leadership protects action. Influence is the discipline of next steps.

Three Short Scenes that Built the Laws

1. **The Quiet Turn in a Noisy Room (Public Speaking)**

   A large hall. Too much movement. I stepped up and did not start with words. I began with a look that said, *We are in the right place. It is safe to arrive.* When I finally spoke, I went straight to one honest story — the boy in the fields learning to listen — and a clear promise: "You will leave today knowing the one sentence your future needs from you." The room gave itself back. It wasn't theatrics. It was alignment: story serving promise, presence serving people.

2. **2) The Reframed Proposal (Sales)**

   A prospective partner wanted features and numbers. I returned the conversation to outcomes and identity: "Tell me the win your people will *feel*, not just the one your spreadsheet will track." We re-scoped the project to what would actually change behavior. The budget didn't shrink; waste did. Sales is stewardship.

3. **3) The Difficult Debrief (Leadership)**

   After a heated season, three trusted leaders told me my style had landed harshly on them. I apologized for my *how*, not my *why*, and I asked, "What would make you feel carried, not just directed?" We agreed on new communication rhythms and kept the standard high. They didn't become softer; we became *stronger* together. Repair turned into redesign.

None of these moments were dramatic. All of them were decisive. They are the everyday places where the TRIAD does its quiet, durable work.

What Changes When You Live the TRIAD

Your calendar stops being a confession of fear. You say fewer yeses with more conviction. Your talks become shorter and land deeper. Your proposals stop begging for approval and start inviting agency. Your teams stop bracing when you walk in and start breathing. You begin to experience the rarest wealth: rooms that get better because you came.

And you start to notice something in the mirror: you are no longer negotiating your worth with the world. You are offering it. That is when influence stops being a tactic and becomes a testimony.

VIII. The Master Law of the Influence TRIAD

Let me put the whole chapter into a single sentence you can carry into any room:

When you speak to move hearts, sell to align decisions, and lead to multiply people, your influence stops chasing attention and starts creating change.

Or, more simply:

Speak to serve. Sell to steward. Lead to lift.

Do this consistently and you will not need to announce your presence. *Results will introduce you.*

A Closing Note to the Builder in You

You did not come from convenience. You came from fields and early mornings and the long obedience of rising. You learned to read weather patterns others ignored. You learned to honor people others overlooked. You learned to repair faster than you are offended. This is your advantage. This is your brand.

So when you step onto a stage — whether it's a hall of thousands or a Tuesday team call — take your sentence with you. Let your story open the door. Let your care clean the air. Let your standard call the best out of people. Then invite them to take the next step you have prepared to hold. That is how Public Speaking becomes more than eloquence, Sales becomes more than conversion, and Leadership becomes more than authority.

And if ever you forget, return to the one line that steadies me wherever I go:

If you are not aware, you are nowhere.
Be here. Be whole. Then move us.

The world is waiting for rooms that feel safer, clearer, and stronger because you arrived. The Influence TRIAD is not a theory. It is the handrail you built with your life. Now let others hold it — and climb.

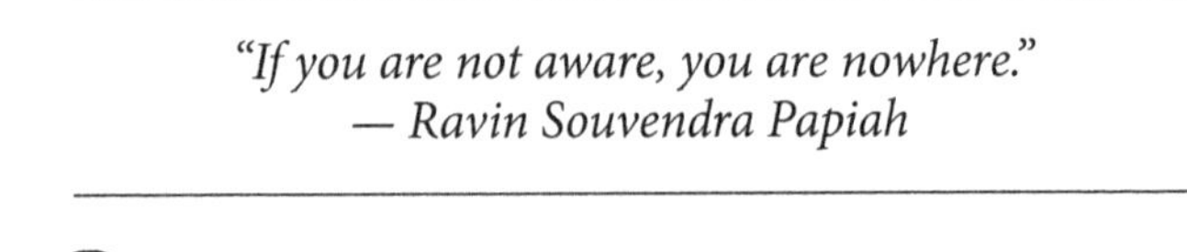

"If you are not aware, you are nowhere."
— Ravin Souvendra Papiah

— *Ravin*

About Ravin

Ravin Souvendra Papiah, CSP, is a leadership strategist, executive coach, and professional speaker based in Mauritius, working with leaders and organisations across Africa, Europe, and global markets. He is the Managing Director of Ravin Papiah Leadership International Ltd, a Certified Speaking Professional (CSP)—the highest internationally recognised designation in professional speaking—Fellow of the Association of Coaching, and a Certified Practitioner of the European Mentoring and Coaching Council (EMCC).

A Distinguished Toastmaster (DTM), Ravin has served in senior leadership roles within Toastmasters International, supporting the development of leaders across multiple countries and cultures. His work sits at the intersection of leadership, communication, and influence, helping executives, entrepreneurs, and high-potential professionals build executive presence, communicate with clarity, and lead confidently in high-stakes moments.

Known for blending lived experience with practical frameworks and compelling storytelling, Ravin's approach is both human and results-driven—rooted in the belief that influence is built through intention, discipline, and courage.

He is also a Fellow of the Chartered Institute of Marketing (FCIM) and of the Mauritius Institute of Directors (FMIoD).

For more about this please visit: https://ravinspapiah.speaka.io/

SESSION TWO

AI

Libby Edmonds

Rainer Petek

Brad Hauck

Fiona Kearns

AI: The New Capability in the Room

If leadership set the tone for the day, then this is the moment the room shifts.

Laptops open.

Questions sharpen.

*And the conversation turns to the tool that is reshaping **how** we work, **how** we lead, and **how** decisions get made.*

Artificial Intelligence has entered the room — not as a future concept, but as a present-day capability.

*This section of the book is not about hype, fear, or technical wizardry. It's about **practical intelligence** — how leaders, businesses, and professionals are actually using AI to extend capacity, improve judgment, and accelerate meaningful outcomes.*

Because AI doesn't replace leadership.

It reveals it.

AI reflects the quality of the questions we ask, the clarity of our intent, and the ethics of our decisions. Used well, it becomes a powerful thinking partner. Used poorly, it simply amplifies confusion at scale.

The chapters in this section cut through the noise and bring the conversation back to what matters. You'll explore how AI can support decision-making, productivity, creativity, and strategic focus — without losing the human insight that makes leadership effective in the first place.

This is not a section for technologists alone.

It's for leaders who understand that AI is no longer optional — but how we integrate it is a choice.

*You'll be invited to think differently about time, leverage, responsibility, and trust. To consider where AI can remove friction — and where human judgment must remain firmly in the loop. And to recognise that the most powerful applications of AI are not about doing **more**, but about doing **what matters** better.*

So stay curious.

Stay grounded.

And stay in the driver's seat.

The future isn't automated.

It's augmented.

Turn the page — the AI conversation starts now.

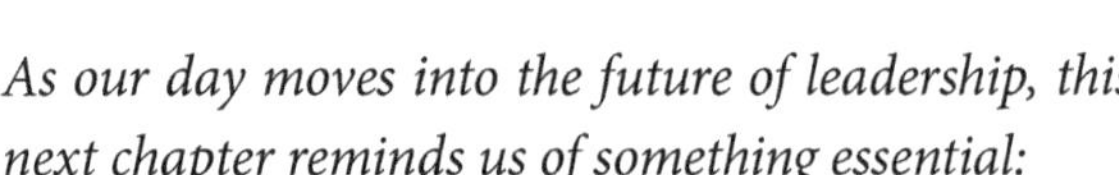

As our day moves into the future of leadership, this next chapter reminds us of something essential:

Technology may be advancing fast — but leadership remains profoundly human.

Introducing Libby Edmonds, South Africa

In *Human-Centred Leadership in the Age of AI*, **Libby Edmonds**, founder of training platform EQlibrium, brings a grounded and practical perspective shaped by decades in education and years working with leaders, teams, and educators across both classrooms and boardrooms.

Libby has seen firsthand that Emotional Intelligence is not a "soft skill" — it is the skill that enables people to navigate uncertainty, strengthen relationships, and lead with clarity, compassion, and purpose. Through her evidence-based **Build Q™ framework**, she shows how leaders can build self-awareness, unlock what holds them back, and design more intentional, human-centered ways of leading and working.

This chapter anchors leadership in what machines cannot replace — awareness, empathy, trust, and choice.

CHAPTER EIGHT

Human-Centered Leadership in the Age of AI

From Control to Connection

School principal Fiona came from a long line of educators, but unlike her father, mother, and generations before her, she once dreamed of a very different future. Brilliant in math and science, she had been fascinated by planes since childhood and longed to study aeronautical engineering. She imagined designing aircraft, breaking barriers, and shaping a life filled with possibility.

But her parents dismissed the idea as unrealistic: *No woman, especially a mother, could do something like that.* The message was clear: ambition had limits. With little encouragement for her aspirations, and pressure to follow the family path, Fiona stepped into teaching — a profession she would eventually grow into, but never truly felt she had chosen.

This unspoken grief shaped her leadership style. She was a tall woman who walked leaning forward — always on a mission, always moving, always trying to keep everything under control. Her curly hair, which she often flattened with the palm of her hand, echoed her lifelong impulse to contain what felt unruly, inside and out.

Fiona was known for her sharp intellect. She could quote policy documents, curriculum frameworks, and data trends with ease. Her meetings were efficient, her reports impeccable, and her results measurable. Yet colleagues rarely felt connected to her. Emotional conversations made her visibly uncomfortable. She struggled with eye contact, often redirecting discussions toward tasks and solutions.

When teachers came to her office with personal concerns, Fiona's instinct was to take charge — to fix, direct, and control. Her anxiety-driven need for order left little room for empathy or collaboration. She connected with her staff through challenge and confrontation rather than curiosity or compassion. Her mantra was often, *"Without me, nothing would get done around here."*

Under her leadership, the school achieved short-term results, but the cost was high. Staff felt silenced, anxious, and emotionally drained. What Fiona saw as efficiency, others experienced as control. Eventually, the school board intervened, and Fiona — reluctantly — agreed to EQ coaching.

That's where her transformation began.

The Paradox of Progress – AI and the Need for EQ

A few months ago, I asked a group of educational leaders, "What word describes how you feel about artificial intelligence?" Their responses — curious, excited, anxious, overwhelmed, fearful, hopeful — revealed one common thread: emotion.

While AI may be artificial, our reactions to it are profoundly human. Behind every wave of technological progress lies uncertainty, awe, and even fear. As AI reshapes how we teach, lead, and connect, it can automate tasks, but it cannot replace trust, judgment, or empathy. Leadership is, and always will be, a deeply human endeavor.

My own journey into Emotional Intelligence began in childhood. I grew up in an environment where emotions were often dismissed or misunderstood. Over time, I discovered that emotions are not weaknesses. They are data, carrying vital information about what matters most. They are primal, universal, functional, and infectious — spreading through our teams and organizations faster than we realize.

Research shows that the emotional state of the leader is the single strongest predictor of a team's success. In an age driven by artificial intelligence, it's *emotional* intelligence that sustains trust, resilience, and connection.

Futurist Jamais Casio says we are living in a BANI world — Brittle, Anxious, Nonlinear, and Incomprehensible. To navigate it, we need leaders who lead with authenticity, empathy, and courage — leaders who are willing to be vulnerable, to invite honest dialogue, and to build trust-centered cultures.

As Joshua Freedman, CEO of Six Seconds Emotional Intelligence Network, reminds us: what we *do* will soon matter less than who we choose to be. Real leadership is tested when the pressure is high and answers are unclear. As automation grows, the most essential human work will be the work of relationships — listening, adapting, caring, and collaborating. The World Economic Forum echoes this truth: emotional intelligence, empathy, resilience, and collaboration are the top skills of the future.

Leadership Rooted in Empathy

Satya Nadella transformed Microsoft's culture by shifting it from internal competition to collaboration. He credits empathy as the turning point in his leadership, stating that "The day I learned empathy was the day I became a leader." Under his guidance, Microsoft's strategy became centered on purpose, accessibility, and human-centered innovation. Nadella consistently promotes the idea that technology should *amplify* human potential, not *replace* it. His leadership demonstrates that emotional intelligence drives innovation more sustainably than efficiency alone.

And that's where Emotional Intelligence (EQ) — and **Build Q**™ — come in.

Redefining Leadership in the AI Era

Leadership used to be defined by authority and expertise. The leader was the one with the answers — the person at the front of the room, the top of the hierarchy, or the head of the table.

But AI has changed that equation. Today, information is everywhere. Answers are one click away. What matters now is not who knows the most, but who can listen deeply, connect authentically, and make decisions that align with human values.

Leadership is no longer about being the smartest person in the room. It's about being the most self-aware.

The best leaders I've met — from school principals to CEOs — share a common trait: they are learners of *themselves*. They reflect on their emotions, question their biases, and seek feedback not to look good, but to *grow* good.

Daniel Goleman, the psychologist who popularized EQ, argues that a leader's emotional state influences the entire organization's mood.

In the AI era, leaders must be intentional about the *energy* they bring into rooms — both physical and virtual. Because while AI can optimize operations, it cannot regulate emotions, resolve conflict, or restore trust. Those are human responsibilities.

Leadership today requires balancing *intelligence* with *integrity,* and *strategy* with *soul.*

And this is where my work in Emotional Intelligence and mental fitness has shown me that great leaders are *builders.* They don't just build businesses; they build *capacity*, *connection*, and *character.*

EQ: The Heart of Leadership

Emotional Intelligence is the ability to understand, manage, and harness emotions — both your own and others' — to guide thinking and behavior effectively.

It is not "soft." It is the new *hard* skill.

In my 30 years as an educator and eight years as an EQ facilitator, I have seen time and again that performance, relationships, and well-being are emotional outcomes. Teams that trust each other perform better. Leaders who demonstrate empathy inspire loyalty. Organizations that align purpose with people are more likely to thrive.

Research from Six Seconds — the global EQ network through which I am a certified practitioner — shows that across the world EQ skills are declining while stress and disconnection are rising. The data calls for a different kind of intelligence — one rooted not in algorithms but in awareness.

When I speak to leaders, I often remark: "AI will never replace emotionally intelligent leaders. But leaders who ignore EQ may well be replaced by those who don't."

The foundation of leadership in this new era is not control, but *consciousness.* It's not about speed, but *self-awareness.*

And that's why I developed **Build Q**™ — a practical roadmap for leaders who want to thrive in a digital age without losing their humanity.

Fiona's Transformation

When Fiona started her EQ coaching journey, she admitted she felt stuck. Her words were sharp, controlled, and precise: "My staff are too emotional. I just need them to focus." But as she completed the *Six Seconds Leadership Self-Assessment*, she began to see what she had never been taught to look at: her own emotions.

The assessment revealed the deeper patterns driving her leadership — her need for control, her discomfort with vulnerability, and the toll of always carrying the weight alone. It became a mirror, not of her failures, but of her possibilities.

Introducing Fiona to the **Build Q**™ Framework marked a turning point — a shift from reaction to reflection, control to connection, ego to purpose.

B — Begin with Self-Awareness

Fiona started noticing her emotional cues — the tight chest, the rising impatience, the instinct to take over. Naming her emotions gave her the first taste of grounded presence.

U — Understand Your Patterns

She recognized how quickly she defaulted to fixing and directing. Pausing before reacting became her new discipline. She began asking herself, "Is this reaction about them — or about me?" This alone softened the atmosphere in her leadership team.

I — Ignite Optimism

Fiona shifted from looking for what was wrong to noticing what was working. She introduced a "celebration minute" in every meeting. Positivity began to take root. Staff started contributing rather than complying.

L — Love Compassionately

This was the deepest stretch. One afternoon a teacher sat in her office in tears, exhausted. Instead of offering solutions, Fiona breathed and said, "I'm here. Tell me what feels heavy." The simple act opened a door to trust. Most importantly, Fiona began a self-compassion mindfulness practice, helping her recognise her inner critic and find greater calm, clarity, and emotional steadiness.

D — Design with Purpose

As Fiona's self-awareness deepened, her vision shifted. She realized her role was not to control outcomes but to create the conditions for others to thrive. She began co-designing initiatives with her heads of department, restoring their autonomy, and inviting their expertise. Leadership became a shared endeavor rather than a personal burden.

Within months, the school's atmosphere began to change. Staff who had once avoided her office began stopping by — not with complaints, but with ideas. Laughter returned to the staffroom. Trust took root. Fiona reflected, "I used to think leadership was about holding everything together. Now I see it's about holding space for others to grow."

Fiona's journey illustrates the intersection of knowledge, wisdom, and trust. Knowledge gave her the skills to lead; wisdom helped her understand herself and others; trust transformed her leadership from control to connection. Her evolution also demonstrates that emotional intelligence is both measurable and learnable — and as we often say, *we can't manage what we don't measure.*

In a world where AI can replicate knowledge, it is this human capacity to feel, reflect, and relate that defines the leaders we remember and the cultures that endure.

Leading AI Integration Through EQ

When the school was challenged to integrate artificial intelligence into its curriculum, Fiona was ready to lead the change. A natural data enthusiast, she was energized by the possibilities AI offered for innovation, creativity, and efficiency. But unlike earlier in her career, her leadership was now grounded in emotional intelligence.

Using the **Build Q™ framework**, she combined her rational and emotional capacities. She used self-awareness to manage uncertainty, understanding to anticipate her team's fears, and compassion to create psychological safety. She facilitated conversations that balanced logic with empathy, helping staff navigate both the technical *and* emotional dimensions of transformation.

The result was a school culture that approached AI not with anxiety, but with curiosity, confidence, and shared purpose. Fiona's evolution demonstrated that sustainable improvement arises when technology and trust, intelligence and empathy work hand in hand — when leaders use both head and heart to design meaningful, human-centered progress.

Sustainable improvement arises when technology and trust, intelligence and empathy work hand in hand — when leaders use both head and heart to design meaningful, human-centered progress.

Knowledge had given Fiona the tools to lead, but emotional intelligence gave her the wisdom to lead with humanity. And it was trust — built through presence, empathy, and authenticity — that moved the school forward.

Key Reflection for Leaders

- Knowledge is what we know. It creates competence.
- Wisdom is how we understand and apply what we know. It creates perspective.
- Trust is how others experience our leadership. It creates a culture where people and ideas grow.

In an era where AI can provide instant knowledge, wisdom and trust remain the uniquely human strengths of transformational leadership.

In a world rapidly shaped by AI, it is this emotional and relational intelligence — the essence of **Build Q**™ — that keeps organizations resilient, human-centered, and ready for the future.

Your Own Journey from Control to Connection

Take a moment to reflect on your own leadership.

- Where might control be limiting collaboration or creativity in your team?
- How might trust open new possibilities for growth and innovation?
- When was the last time you truly listened — not to fix, but to understand?

Real leadership is not about managing every outcome. It's about creating space where others can thrive.

Ask yourself: *What could shift if I led with a little less control and a little more connection?*

Build Q™ in Action: From Concept to Practice

1. **B – Begin with Self-Awareness:**
   Schedule five minutes of stillness daily. Reflect on one emotion you felt strongly that day — what triggered it and how you responded.

2. **U – Understand Patterns**
   Keep a "leadership journal." Track recurring moments of frustration or joy. Patterns reveal values.

3. **I – Ignite Optimism:**
   Start meetings with a question: *"What's one thing that's going well?"* It shifts collective focus toward solutions.

4. **L – Love Compassionately**
   In one-on-one check-ins, don't just ask *"What are you working on?"* but *"How are you doing?"*

5. **D – Design with Purpose:**
   Revisit your mission statement. Does it still inspire you? How can AI and innovation serve that deeper purpose?

Each of these steps builds new neural pathways. And like physical fitness, mental and emotional fitness strengthen through practice.

Conclusion: Building the Future with Heart and Intelligence

We are living through one of the greatest transitions in human history. AI will continue to learn faster — but humans must learn *deeper.*

The leaders who will shape the future are those who integrate both head and heart, algorithm and empathy, data and dignity.

Leadership is not about being perfect. It's about being *present*. It's about showing up with awareness, compassion, and courage — and inspiring others to do the same.

The **Build Q**™ model reminds us that as we build organizations, we are also building ourselves.

We are building understanding, optimism, love, and purpose.

We are building trust in a time of uncertainty.

We are building the bridge between artificial and emotional intelligence.

"Emotions drive people and people drive performance"
— Six Seconds

"We can teach machines to think faster, but it is our emotional intelligence that teaches us to lead with wisdom and earn trust." — Libby Edmonds

---

— Libby

The Build Q™ Leadership Checklist

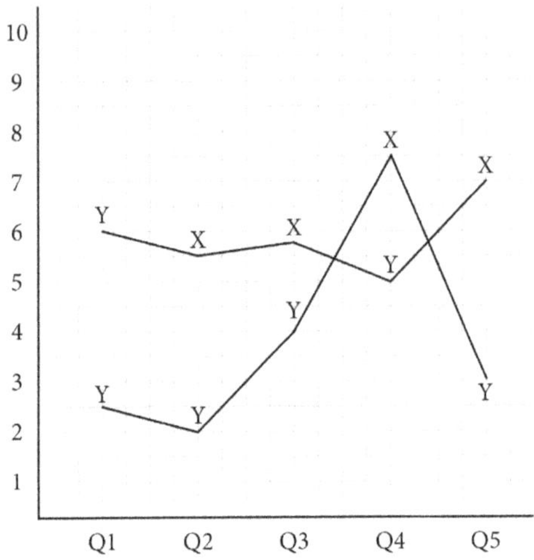

Step 1: On a scale of 1-10 rank where you think you are for each of the 5 quick questions. Mark with an (X)

Step 2: Now, on a scale of 1-10 rank where your team members percieve you are for each of those. Mark with a (Y)

5 Quick Questions

Begin with Self-Awareness

1. Do I regularly pause to reflect on my emotions, energy, and the impact I have on others —especially before high-stakes conversations or decisions?

Understand Your Patterns and Triggers

2. Have I identified any recurring emotional patterns or automatic reactions in my leadership, and how do I consciously shift them to be more effective and compassionate?

Ignite Optimism

3. In times of challenge or uncertainty, do I focus on what's possible and inspire a hopeful, forward-looking mindset within my team?

Love Compassionately

4. Do I lead with empathy and geunine care — valuing people not just for what they do, but for who they are?

Design with Purpose

5. Are my decisions and actions aligned with clear values, shared meaning, and long-term human-centred goals — not just short-term outcomes?

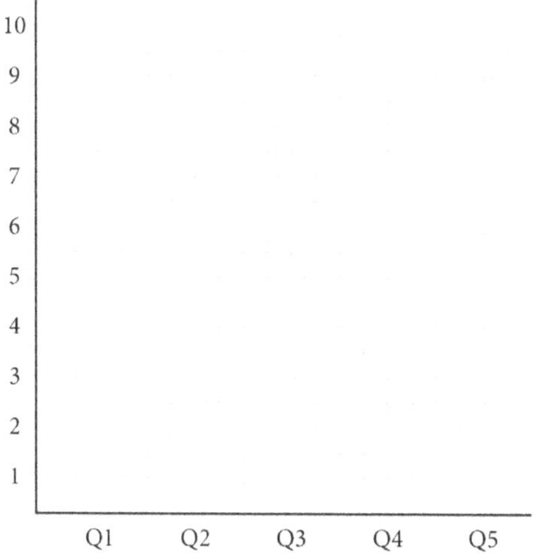

Scan the QR code to download the extended version of your **Build Q™** *Leadership* **Checklist***. 5 quick questions, Rate your* **Build Q™** *skills as a leader.*

www.eqlibrium.co.za

About Libby

Libby Edmonds is the founder of Eqlibrium, the architect of the **Build Q**™ philosophy, a certified Emotional Intelligence facilitator, and mental fitness and leadership coach who helps leaders and teams turn emotional insight into enduring, observable change.

Through her **Build Q**™ framework, Libby equips individuals and organizations to build resilience, deepen trust, and create sustainable, human-centered cultures. Her mission is simple: to help leaders develop the emotional capacity required not just to perform, but to lead with courage, curiosity and collaboration.

With decades of experience as an educator and more than ten years facilitating emotional learning in environments ranging from classrooms to boardrooms, and with the benefit of her lived experience, Libby has seen how EQ and **Build Q**™ change the way people lead, relate, and decide under pressure. In a world defined by uncertainty, Emotional Intelligence is no longer optional: it is the core leadership capability.

Libby challenges leaders worldwide to move beyond awareness toward intentional action by using her 5 **Build Q**™ science-based competencies to form teams that lead with empathy, accountability, and measurable results.

Ladies and gentlemen, what you're about to read isn't theory. It's survival knowledge from someone who made a choice 250 meters up a vertical wall: adapt or fall.

Introducing Rainer Petek CSP, Global Speaking Fellow, Germany

Rainer Petek conquered the Alps' most notorious North Faces before most of us finished university. Today, as a Global Speaking Fellow and current president of the German Speakers Association, he has transformed leadership thinking across 30 countries. He brings us something unprecedented: a framework for partnering with AI that doesn't replace human judgment — it amplifies it.

If you've ever felt paralyzed by the pace of change or wondered how to lead when the old playbook is obsolete, this chapter is your new safety rope. Welcome Rainer Petek — and the revolution of the Human-Machine Rope Team.

CHAPTER NINE

The Human-Machine Rope Team

Leading at the Edge of the Unknown

The Moment of Truth

Two hundred and fifty meters up the overhanging rocks of the Yellow Edge on the Cima Piccola in the Dolomites, I stood on a ledge barely wide enough for the balls of my feet. Beneath my heels: nothing but air. Above me: an overhang I couldn't see past. Behind me: an irreversible climbing move that meant no retreat. My strength: enough for maybe only three minutes.

I knew exactly how this would end if I didn't move. The mathematics were simple and brutal. Ten meters above my last belay point, a fall would mean 20 meters down, plus another 5 meters of rope stretch.

A 25-meter pendulum swing into the vertical face. Probably surviv-able, definitely humiliating, certainly the end of this climb.

But here's what changed everything: I stopped looking down and started looking at what I was *really* looking at — my own thought patterns. *I can't do this*, my inner dialogue insisted. *This is impossible. I will fall. Maybe I should just jump and get it over with.* I caught myself mid-spiral and recognized something crucial: I was watching myself think. And what I was thinking was destroying me faster than gravity ever could.

So I did something counterintuitive. Despite every instinct screaming to cling tighter to the rock, I leaned back. I extended my arms fully, pushed away from the wall, and looked up. That simple shift — maybe 50 centimeters of physical distance — changed my entire world. Suddenly I could see over the overhang. There were holds up there. Good ones. And beyond them, a crack system that would lead back to the original route.

I took a breath and began an instructive dialogue with myself: *Right hand up. Good. Left hand up. Now right foot. Step. Yes.* Each small action that worked built confidence for the next. Within three minutes, I was safe at a solid stance, building an anchor, bringing Thomas, my rope partner, up behind me.

That was 1983. I was eighteen years old. And while I didn't know it then, I was learning the fundamental skill that leaders need most today: how to navigate terrain where the old routes don't exist and the new ones aren't marked.

The Digital Overhang

Today, as leaders, we are all hanging on that ledge. The overhang above us is no longer made of Dolomite limestone; it is the opaque, rapidly accelerating canopy of the rise of artificial intelligence.

In my work with leadership teams across the world, I hear the same exhausted refrain: "We know we need to transform. We know

AI changes everything and we should think strategically. But we're already running at 110%. How can we plan when everything might be different tomorrow? How can we show confidence when we genuinely don't know what's coming?"

The traditional leadership model — Vision, Analysis, Plan, Execute, Review — assumed you could separate these activities in time. Strategic planning happened at annual offsites. Execution happened during the year. Review happened quarterly. That sequential model is dead. The terrain is changing faster than the time between your planning sessions.

But here's what most leadership writing gets wrong: They tell you to "embrace uncertainty" or "be agile" without giving you an actual framework for *how*. Or they give you AI tools without helping you understand the fundamental shift in what leadership means when you're no longer climbing alone.

The Human-Machine Rope Team

In mountaineering, we survive by forming a *Seilschaft*, a rope team. What if you approached AI the same way and built a "Human–Machine Rope Team?" The AI is the partner that secures us, augments our reach, and processes the data. But we remain the lead climbers. We decide the route. We take the risk. We define the meaning.

Use AI not as a tool when convenient. Not as automation that replaces thinking. But as a *rope partner* — a companion with fundamentally different capabilities that, when properly integrated with your human judgment, enables you to navigate terrain that neither of you could handle alone.

Your AI rope partner brings superhuman speed, tireless pattern recognition across millions of data points, scenario generation at scale, 24/7 vigilance for weak signals, and no emotional attachment to past decisions.

You bring ethical judgment, contextual wisdom, emotional intelligence, relationship trust, intuitive leaps, moral courage, and the willingness to be accountable.

The magic happens in the integration. But like any rope team, it requires practice, clear communication, and understanding that you're still the leader. The AI doesn't climb for you. It climbs *with* you.

The Four-Field Framework for AI-Augmented Leadership

That day on the Yellow Edge taught me something that took years to fully articulate: successful navigation of uncertainty requires holding two tensions simultaneously, not sequentially.

The Vertical Tension: You need clarity about both the *future* (where you're trying to go) and the *present* (the reality you're in right now).

The Horizontal Tension: You need both *action* (decisive movement despite uncertainty) and *reflection* (the strategic pause to see what you're missing).

Today's leader needs real-time integration of all four fields. Here's how the human–machine rope team transforms each field into solid anchor points that help you navigate the right route, even when everything changes in an instant.

Field One: FUTURE - The Good Enough Vision

On that ledge, I had an ambition for the future: I wanted to become an extreme climber. That ambition gave me courage when panic set in. *This is exactly what I came here for*, I reminded myself. But I didn't have a perfect plan. I had direction.

Traditional leadership says: Develop a crystal-clear three-year strategic plan.

AI-augmented leadership says: Create a "direction corridor" with multiple scenario paths, refreshed continuously.

The Human–Machine Partnership:

Your AI rope partner can generate 20 future scenarios based on current market signals in 10 minutes. It can synthesize competitive intelligence, technological trends, demographic shifts, and regulatory changes across industries and geographies at a scale that is impossible for any human team.

But AI cannot answer the questions that matter most: Which scenarios align with our values? Which future do we want to create? What are we willing to sacrifice to get there? That's human work.

In Practice: A manufacturing CEO I work with uses this approach. Every Monday morning, she asks her AI partner: "Based on last week' s data — customer conversations, competitor moves, technology announcements — what scenarios should we be considering?" The AI generates five scenarios. She and her team choose which two to explore deeply, based on their strategic intent and values. And then they stress-test their current initiatives against both scenarios.

"I don't need perfect prediction," she told me. "I need my team mentally prepared for multiple futures. AI makes that possible without burning everyone out in endless planning sessions."

The Principle: Direction beats precision. A good enough vision, continuously refreshed, beats a perfect plan that's obsolete before it's implemented.

Field Two: PRESENT - Honest Reality Assessment

When I leaned back from the wall, I could clearly assess my real situation. Not my fears. Not my hopes. Reality. I was off route. I had limited strength. But I also had options I couldn't see when I was plastered against the rock, paralyzed by proximity to the problem.

Traditional leadership says: Monthly dashboards, quarterly business reviews.

AI-augmented leadership says: Real-time peripheral vision, with human interpretation.

The Human–Machine Partnership:
Your AI rope partner can monitor signals you'd never track manually: subtle shifts in customer sentiment across thousands of interactions, emerging competitor patterns, internal bottlenecks showing up in communication flows, early warnings in supply chain data.

But AI cannot interpret what these signals *mean* for your specific context. Is this signal or noise? Is this an opportunity — or a distraction? What's the real risk here? That requires human judgment, shaped by experience and intuition.

In Practice: A healthcare technology firm uses AI to monitor customer support conversations in real-time. The AI flags when language patterns shift — when customers stop asking "How do I do X?" and start asking "Why can't I do Y?" That shift signals unmet needs before they show up in churn data.

But the CEO makes the call on which signals to act on: "AI showed us that nurses were asking different questions than administrators using the same product. We'd have missed that in traditional surveys. But deciding to build separate interfaces for each role — that was a human decision based on our mission to serve frontline healthcare workers."

The Principle: On the Yellow Edge, I assessed the risk of non-change (falling because my strength ran out) versus the risk of change (falling while trying to climb). The risk of action was actually lower. AI helps you see that analysis more clearly, faster, and with better data. But you make the call.

Field Three: ACTION - Learning While Moving

Once I decided to move, something fascinating happened. My internal dialogue shifted from destructive to instructive: "Right hand up. Left hand up. Right foot step. Stand." Each successful micro-action built confidence for the next. I wasn't thinking about the whole route anymore. Just the next move.

Traditional leadership says: Plan thoroughly, then execute with discipline.

AI-augmented leadership says: Create "places for the new" where you can experiment, learn, and iterate at speed.

The Human–Machine Partnership:
Your AI rope partner can help you prototype experiments, simulate outcomes, and test variations before you commit resources. It can help you design minimal viable interventions.

But AI cannot bring the customer empathy that turns a technical experiment into a breakthrough. It cannot make the ethical judgment calls about what's safe-to-fail versus reckless.

In Practice: A financial services leader used this approach when his team wanted to redesign their customer onboarding. Instead of a nine-month waterfall project, they defined five "places for the new" — specific customer segments where they could try different approaches safely.

"Before each experiment, I'd ask my personal AI to stress-test it against 10 scenarios: What if customers react this way? What if regulators question that? What if our legacy systems can't handle the integration?" he explained. "It didn't replace real-world testing. It made our tests smarter and faster. We learned in six weeks what would have taken a year of traditional piloting."

The Principle: External orientation beats internal targets. Watch what actually happens with real customers, not what your plan predicted. AI helps you watch more broadly and learn more quickly. You decide what the learning means and where to go next.

Field Four: REFLECTION - Strategic Timeouts in Real-Time

The moment I leaned back from the wall was a moment of forced reflection. I had to literally detach from the problem to see it clearly. That 50-centimeter shift in perspective revealed options invisible from up close.

Traditional leadership says: Annual strategy offsites, maybe quarterly retreats.

AI-augmented leadership says: Daily strategic alignment, weekly perspective shifts, continuous pattern recognition.

The Human–Machine Partnership:
Your AI rope partner makes an extraordinary sparring mate because it never gets tired, never judges, and can hold complexity without reducing it to false simplicity. You can "think out loud" with AI during strategic timeouts. It will surface contradictions in your thinking, ask clarifying questions, connect dots across domains you'd never link.

But AI cannot synthesize insights into wisdom, nor can it feel the intuitive tug toward an emerging possibility. That's human territory.

In Practice: I personally use this every Friday afternoon. I block 90 minutes, labeled "Strategic Timeout" on my calendar. No meetings. Phone off. I review the week's significant moments, and then I dialogue with my personal AI: "Here' s what I observed this week about client needs, market shifts, and internal patterns. What am I not seeing? What contradicts what? Where are the weak signals I might be missing?"

Sometimes the AI surfaces nothing useful. Sometimes it asks a question that cracks open my thinking: "You mentioned three different clients asking about implementation speed. You said it was about their impatience. But could it be about their budget cycles?" That shift in perspective led to a complete redesign of how I package my services.

The Principle: You must detach from the problem to solve the problem. Proximity creates blindness. AI can help you zoom out (see patterns across all your data) and zoom in (examine granular details you'd miss) with deliberate intention. But you bring the discernment about which zoom level matters right now.

The Real-Time Integration Challenge

Here's where it gets transformational. Because AI operates at machine speed, the real-time integration of all four fields becomes achievable for the first time in leadership history.

Your AI rope partner can:

- Track your strategic vision while simultaneously scanning for present reality shifts

- Suggest action experiments while you're still in reflection mode

- Connect patterns across all four fields that would be invisible to human bandwidth

But you remain the leader — the one who decides, who takes responsibility, who brings human wisdom to machine capability.

On the Yellow Edge, I had to integrate all four fields in about 90 seconds: reconnect with my ambition (becoming an extreme climber); assess present reality honestly (the routes, the risks); decide on action (climb up those holds); and maintain reflective awareness throughout (monitoring my internal dialogue, watching for new information).

Today's leaders need that same integration, but continuously. The difference? You're not alone anymore. You have a rope partner who never sleeps, never stops seeing patterns, never gets overwhelmed by data volume.

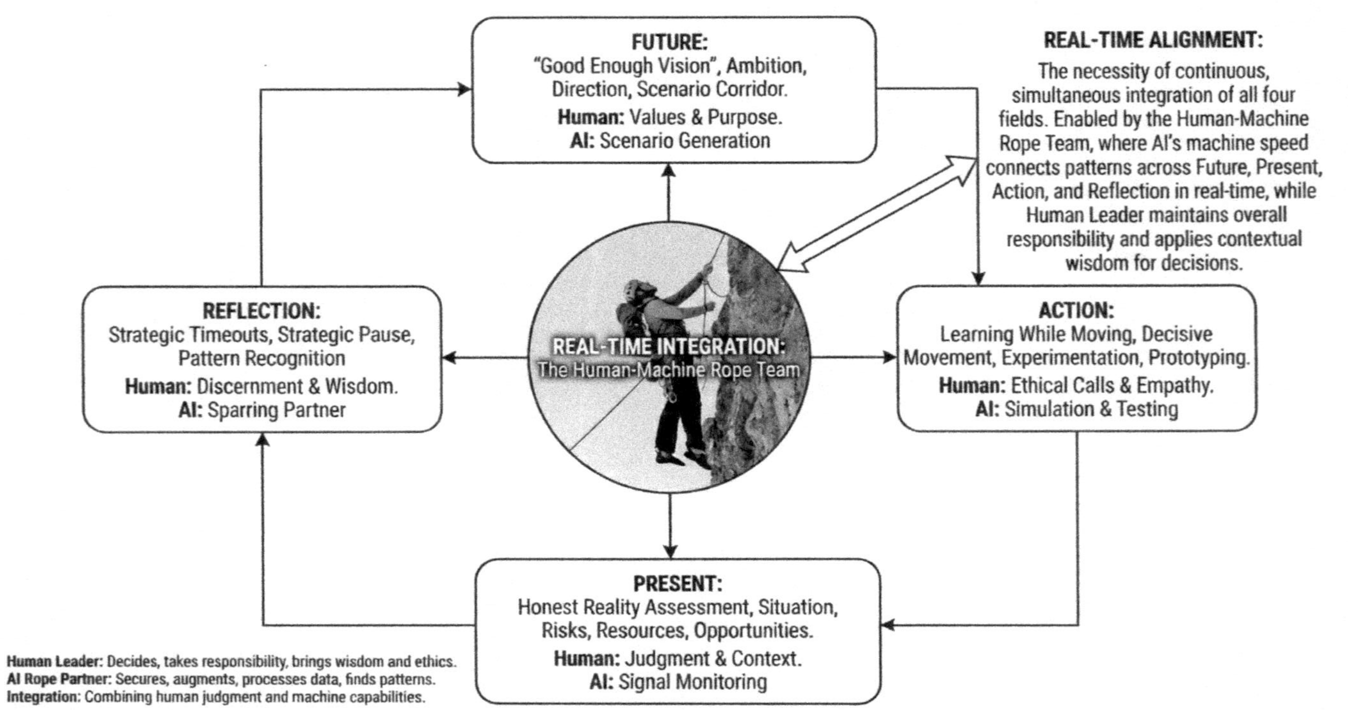

FUTURE:
"Good Enough Vision", Ambition, Direction, Scenario Corridor.
Human: Values & Purpose.
AI: Scenario Generation

REAL-TIME ALIGNMENT:
The necessity of continuous, simultaneous integration of all four fields. Enabled by the Human-Machine Rope Team, where AI's machine speed connects patterns across Future, Present, Action, and Reflection in real-time, while Human Leader maintains overall responsibility and applies contextual wisdom for decisions.

REFLECTION:
Strategic Timeouts, Strategic Pause, Pattern Recognition
Human: Discernment & Wisdom.
AI: Sparring Partner

REAL-TIME INTEGRATION:
The Human-Machine Rope Team

ACTION:
Learning While Moving, Decisive Movement, Experimentation, Prototyping.
Human: Ethical Calls & Empathy.
AI: Simulation & Testing

PRESENT:
Honest Reality Assessment, Situation, Risks, Resources, Opportunities.
Human: Judgment & Context.
AI: Signal Monitoring

Human Leader: Decides, takes responsibility, brings wisdom and ethics.
AI Rope Partner: Secures, augments, processes data, finds patterns.
Integration: Combining human judgment and machine capabilities.

The Inner Game of Leadership

Here's the paradox: As AI becomes more capable, the premium on distinctly human leadership qualities skyrockets. Especially when you want — and need — the buy-in from your team.

Back then in the '90s, when I asked Ludwig, my longtime climbing client, what motivated him to follow me as his mountain guide, he said something that changed how I understand leadership: "You burn for climbing yourself. That passion is infectious. You set challenging goals, and that pushes me beyond what I thought possible. It's never about your personal glory — always about our shared success. And you're constantly aware of conditions, risks, and weather. I trust your judgment because you're paying attention to what matters."

Research by organizational psychologist Robert Quinn identifies **four qualities that make people choose to follow a leader** (think of following not as waiting for instructions, but as the willingness to bring the best ideas, efforts, and contributions to work):

1. **Ambitious:** Are you pursuing meaningful challenges, not just maintaining comfort?

2. **Integrity-driven:** Are you focused on collective success, not personal advantage?

3. **Values-grounded:** Are you consistent when conditions get uncomfortable?

4. **Openly aware:** Are you perceiving signals others miss, staying curious and adaptive?

In the AI age, these human qualities matter more than ever. Because AI can make you faster, but not wiser. AI can show you patterns, but not purpose. AI can generate options, but cannot make the call.

The New Leadership Muscle is developed by (a) knowing when to lean on your AI rope partner and when to trust your inner voice;

and (b) knowing when to accept AI-generated insights and when to override them based on contextual wisdom AI cannot access.

This requires new inner work:

- **Humility:** Accepting that AI knows more facts while you bring better judgment.
- **Curiosity:** Constantly asking "What can my AI partner help me see?"
- **Discipline:** Not outsourcing thinking but augmenting it.
- **Responsibility:** Knowing you cannot blame AI for your decisions.

Working on yourself *is* the leadership work. When your team sees you combining AI-enhanced insights with human wisdom and care, they'll trust you. The machine makes you smarter. You make the machine meaningful.

Where to Start Monday

If you're reading this and thinking, *This sounds great, but where do I actually begin?* — here's your start:

This Week:

1. Choose your AI rope partner for strategic dialogue (e.g., Claude, ChatGPT, or similar).
2. Schedule your first strategic timeout: 60–90 minutes, Friday afternoon.
3. Bring one real challenge to that timeout and "think out loud" with your AI partner.
4. Ask: "Based on what I just described, what am I not seeing?"
5. Notice: What feels helpful versus what feels hollow?

This Month:

1. Map your four fields (Present, Future, Action, and Reflection): Where are you strongest? Where are you dangerously weak?

2. For each field, ask: Where could AI increase my capability 10X? Where must I remain fully human?

3. Identify one "place for the new": What's a safe-to-fail experiment you could run this quarter?

4. Define your "places of silence": Where can you go periodically to hear your inner voice?

5. Set your boundaries: What will you never delegate to AI? Write it down.

This Quarter:

- Daily: Identify one strategic question to ask your AI rope partner.

- Weekly: Practice one AI-assisted perspective shift exercise.

- Monthly: Have a team conversation about AI-augmented four-field practice.

A warning: Just like on a mountain, a rope team only works with practice, communication, and clear roles. Don't expect magic on day one. Expect partnership built over time.

The Invitation to Rope Up

Back on that ledge at the Yellow Edge, I was alone — just me, the rock, and gravity. I had to find the answer within myself. Today's leaders don't have to be alone.

You have the most capable thinking partner in human history ready to rope up with you. But here's the truth that most AI hype misses:

AI won't lead. You lead.

AI won't decide. You decide

AI won't take responsibility. You do.

What AI *will* do:

- See patterns you'd miss across millions of data points.
- Generate options you wouldn't imagine in available time.
- Work tirelessly alongside you without fatigue.
- Challenge your assumptions without ego.
- Amplify your best thinking without replacing it.

But this happens only if you treat it as a rope partner, not a tool. Only if you learn to climb together. Only if you maintain the real-time integration of future vision, present reality, decisive action, and strategic reflection.

Remember: Present, Future, Action, and Reflection. This four-field framework gives you the map. AI gives you enhanced capabilities to navigate all four fields simultaneously. But you — your judgment, your values, your leadership — you're still the guide.

Your move, leader. The rope is there. The terrain is changing. The question is simple:

Will you clip in?

— Rainer

About Rainer

Rainer Petek, CSP, Global Speaking Fellow and President of the German Speakers Association, is redefining leadership for the AI age. At 18, he conquered the notorious Yellow Edge on the Cima Piccola — 250 meters of overhanging rock where a single wrong move meant a 25-meter fall. That experience taught him what most leadership books miss: the future belongs to those who can integrate vision, reality, action, and reflection in real-time, not in sequence.

Today, Rainer translates extreme mountaineering survival strategies into frameworks for navigating radical business uncertainty. As trusted advisor, sought-after keynote speaker, and founding partner of 3U Leaders, he has guided C-suite executives across more than 30 countries through their own "digital overhangs" — moments where the old routes no longer exist and the new ones aren't yet visible.

His breakthrough **Human-Machine Rope Team** framework teaches leaders to partner with AI as a strategic ally rather than merely a tool — combining machine-speed pattern recognition with irreplaceable human judgment. With 10 published books, 25+ years as a trusted advisor for leaders, and 35+ years as a certified mountain guide, Rainer brings a rare combination: the adrenaline of life-or-death decision-making and the pragmatic rigor of systemic organizational development. He doesn't just theorize about uncertainty. He has survived it at altitude — and teaches you to thrive in it at scale.

For more about this please visit: https://rainerpetek.com

Our next chapter turns up the pace, this is the moment in the day when leaders are asked to stop watching change — and start positioning ahead of it.

Introducing Brad Hauck, Australia

In *Ahead of the Curve,* **Brad Hauck** draws on decades of experience in digital transformation and frontline firefighting to deliver a powerful message: reacting is no longer enough. In a world where change accelerates exponentially, leadership is about anticipation, preparation, and decisive action.

Using vivid real-world analogies and practical insight, Brad challenges leaders to rethink how they assess risk, build capability, and prepare their teams before disruption hits. This chapter is not about panic — it's about positioning.

Because when the fire moves faster than you can run, the leaders who survive are the ones who were already moving.

CHAPTER TEN

Ahead of the Curve

Embracing AI Leadership

When the Fire Moves Faster Than You Can Run

For over 20 years, I've served as a volunteer rural firefighter in Australia, responding to hundreds of wildfires and other emergencies. In that role, I've learned something that most people don't truly understand until they've faced it: fire moves faster than you think, faster than you plan for, and often faster than you can react to.

There's a concept in firefighting called *the dead man's zone*. Just as deadly as it sounds, it's the distance a wildfire can travel in five minutes. It's the area directly in front of an active fire where, if you're caught, you have almost no chance of survival. The fire moves with such ferocity that your only option is to be somewhere else already. You can't outrun it once you're in that zone. Survival depends on anticipating where the fire will be, not understanding where it is now.

I've watched AI transform the business landscape with the same terrifying speed, and the parallel is uncanny: **organizations that wait to react until they can see the flames are already in the dead man's zone. By the time the threat is obvious, it's too late to escape.**

The leaders who survive — in firefighting and in business — aren't the ones who react fastest. They're the ones who read the conditions, anticipate movement, and position themselves ahead of the fire line before the critical moment arrives.

A Front-Row Seat to Multiple Firestorms

My relationship with rapid, unstoppable change isn't theoretical. I've lived it in two parallel worlds that have shaped how I think about leadership and survival.

In one world, I'm suited up in protective gear, coordinating teams to contain wildfires that can jump firebreaks, change direction without warning, and consume everything in their path. I've seen fires travel hundreds of meters in minutes. I've witnessed the split-second difference between a controlled burn and a catastrophe. I've stood at the edge of landscapes transformed beyond recognition in hours.

In the other world — digital marketing — I've spent 25 years watching technological wildfires reshape entire industries: from telecommunications to the birth of the internet, from the web revolution to Google's dominance, from social media to AI. I've been on the front lines as each wave of innovation consumed the old and created entirely new paradigms.

Under the right conditions, change accelerates exponentially, and what seemed manageable yesterday becomes overwhelming today.

Both experiences taught me the same fundamental truth: speed is not constant. **Under the right conditions, change accelerates exponentially, and what seemed manageable yesterday becomes overwhelming today.**

The internet took approximately seven years to reach 100 million users. Facebook achieved it in about four years. Instagram did it in two and a half years. Then ChatGPT shattered every expectation by reaching 100 million users in *two months*. That's the fastest adoption curve of any consumer technology in human history.[1]

By August 2024, research from Harvard economists revealed that nearly 40% of U.S. adults aged 18–64 had used generative AI. That adoption rate significantly outpaced both the personal computer (20% after three years) and the internet (20% after two years) over the same timeframe.[2]

This isn't a normal technology adoption curve. This is a firestorm, and the conditions are perfect for it to accelerate even more.

Why This Time Is Different

Any experienced firefighter will tell you that the fire itself isn't what makes a situation catastrophic; it's the conditions. Wind, temperature, humidity, fuel load, and terrain can combine to create conditions where a manageable burn becomes an unstoppable wall of flame.

We're in those conditions *now* with AI.

The "fuel load": Decades of digitized data, computing infrastructure, cloud platforms, and internet connectivity have been building for years.

---

1   https://www.reuters.com/technology/chatgpt-sets-record-fastest-growing-user-base-analyst-note-2023-02-01/

2   https://news.harvard.edu/gazette/story/2024/10/generative-ai-embraced-faster-than-internet-pcs/
https://news.harvard.edu/gazette/story/2024/10/generative-ai-embraced-faster-than-internet-pcs/

The "wind": Massive investment, open-source development, and competitive pressure are pushing AI development at unprecedented speeds.

The "temperature": Market demand, productivity pressure, and fear of being left behind have never been greater.

When I look at how technology has progressed during my digital marketing career, I can see the conditions intensifying.

- **1990s**: The internet connects universities and early adopters (small, controlled burns).
- **Late 1990s**: The web makes the internet visual and accessible (fire spreads to new fuel).
- **Early 2000s**: Content management systems democratize website creation (the wind picks up).
- **Mid 2000s**: Google organizes the world's information (our fire jumps the first major firebreak).
- **2010s**: Mobile and social media put the internet in everyone's pocket (conditions become extreme).
- **2020s**: AI transforms from tool to collaborator (the firestorm begins).

Each phase has happened faster than the previous one, and each innovation has created more fuel for the next. Now we're watching something I've seen in both firefighting and technology: **exponential acceleration that defies linear thinking.**

Most people think "exponentially" means "really fast." But it's more than that. Exponential means the rate of change itself is accelerating. The distance the fire travels in the next five minutes is greater than the distance it traveled in the previous five minutes — and the distance after that is greater still. Momentum kicks in.

This is why organizations that plan based on last year's pace of change are already in the dead man's zone. They're using yesterday's fire to predict tomorrow's firestorm.

You Can't Fight Fire by Chasing It

In my career, I've had two profound wake-up calls that taught me the same lesson from different angles. Both times, I learned that trying to catch up to something moving faster than you can react is a losing strategy.

The first happened during my master's research. I set out to write a thesis on creating educational websites, which was a very forward-thinking topic in the early 2000s. The premise was solid. I'd explore best practices for building effective educational web platforms for school students, but within a single academic year, the entire landscape transformed. Text-based websites gave way to rich multimedia experiences. Video streaming was no longer a novelty; it was an expectation. What students did online changed so dramatically that my original question became obsolete before I was halfway through writing my thesis.

I had to pivot completely. The thesis evolved from "how to make educational websites" to "how students research online" because the technology, behaviors, and usage had changed faster than I could document them. It was like trying to paint a landscape while a wildfire was actively consuming it. *By the time I painted where the fire was going, it was already somewhere else entirely.*

If you're always reacting to where the fire just was, you'll never stop it from consuming what's ahead.

The second wake-up call came more recently, while watching colleagues and businesses struggle with the AI revolution. People were trying to master yesterday's version of technology while tomorrow's version was already being deployed. They were chasing the fire line instead of anticipating where it would move next.

This is the uncomfortable truth that keeps business leaders awake at night: **if you're always reacting to where the fire just was, you'll never stop it from consuming what's ahead.**

In firefighting, we call this *chasing your tail*. It's exhausting, demoralizing, and futile. The only way to contain a wildfire is to anticipate its movement, get ahead of it, and create containment lines where it's going, not where it's been.

The same principle applies to AI adoption. There is no point trying to catch up by mastering last year's tools while this year's tools are already transforming industries. To do so is to chase your tail and get buried in the process.

What Firefighting Taught Me about Leadership in the AI Era

Twenty years of firefighting has radically shaped how I think about leadership, risk, and survival in ways that directly apply to business disruption. Let me share the principles that have kept me alive in wildfires *and* thriving through years of technological change:

1. Respect the Exponential

The most dangerous type of firefighter is the one who underestimates fire conditions. I've seen experienced crews get caught because they assessed their risk based on simple thinking: *If the fire is here and moving at this speed, we have X amount of time.* They forget that under extreme conditions fire doesn't always move linearly. It accelerates. It jumps. It creates its own weather.

The AI we're seeing now is showing the same exponential behavior. The *Financial Times* [3] confirmed that AI penetration into businesses is growing at rates that dwarf the adoption curve of the early internet—not by small percentages but by huge jumps.

---

3   https://www.tomshardware.com/tech-industry/ai-adoption-far-outpaces-that-of-the-early-internet-report-sheds-light-on-worldwide-ai-penetration-and-usage-patterns

Most business leaders are still thinking linearly: *AI is advancing quickly, so we'll reassess in six months.* But six months from now, the capability gap between AI adopters and non-adopters won't be 10 percent wider; it could be 10x wider. The models will be more capable, the tools more accessible, the competitive advantages more entrenched.

You need to act now. If you wait until you're fully comfortable, you're already in the dead man's zone.

2. Position Beats Reaction Speed

I'm not the fastest firefighter. I'm not the strongest or the youngest, but I'm still here after 20 years because I've learned that positioning beats speed every time. If you're in the right place before the critical moment arrives, you don't need to be fast. If you're in the wrong position, even the speed of an Olympian won't save you.

In business, I see too many leaders obsessing over speed of implementation — "We need to deploy AI faster! Train teams faster! Execute faster!"—all while ignoring strategic positioning. They're trying to outrun a fire instead of positioning themselves where the fire can't hurt them.

When AI disruption comes to your industry — and it will — the survival of your business won't depend on how fast you can react in that moment. It will depend on the choices you made months or years ago.

Strategically positioning yourself in the AI era means:

- Building AI literacy across your organization *before* you need specific solutions

- Creating processes and workflows that can incorporate AI tools as they emerge

- Developing relationships with AI consultants, vendors, and thought leaders before problems hit
- Fostering a culture that embraces change rather than resists it

When AI disruption comes to your industry — and it will — the survival of your business won't depend on how fast you can react in that moment. It will depend on the choices you made months or years ago.

3. Know When to Backburn

In firefighting, sometimes the best way to stop a wildfire is to intentionally burn the fuel ahead of it. We call this a *backburn*. Lighting a fire to stop a fire might sound odd, but it works because you're removing the fuel the wildfire needs to keep burning.

In business, it means *strategically disrupting yourself before change disrupts you.* It means identifying which of your current processes, revenue streams, or competitive advantages may be affected by AI and proactively improving or replacing them even when they're still profitable today.

I've seen this play out repeatedly in digital marketing. The SEO strategies that generated over $1 billion in revenue for my clients over the years? Many of them have had to be abandoned now, not because they stopped working but because AI-powered techniques worked better. I also had to backburn my own expertise to stay ahead of the fire line and deliver results for my clients. This is sometimes difficult because it requires burning what's valuable now to protect what will be valuable tomorrow. But the alternative is waiting for AI to make the decision for you when you're least prepared. One path gives you control; the other leaves you scrambling to save your business.

4. Clear Communication under Pressure Saves Lives

In a wildfire, communication breakdowns are disastrous. When conditions are changing rapidly, teams are fatigued, and visibility is poor, the crews that are safest are the ones that maintain clear channels of communication.

I've watched too many businesses fail at adopting AI, not because they lacked tools or resources but because their leaders couldn't communicate clearly about *what* was happening, *why* it mattered, and what was *expected* of their teams.

Your people are watching you right now. They see AI everywhere, and they're probably already using it in their everyday lives. But they're uncertain about job security and anxious about whether their skills will remain relevant. Your silence creates a vacuum that fills them with fear and inspires rumors.

The leaders who are working through this transition successfully don't have all the answers, but they communicate with clarity, honesty, and consistency. Their messaging is:

- "Here's what we know about AI's impact on our industry."
- "Here's what we're uncertain about and how we're learning more."
- "Here's what we're doing to position the organization for success."
- "Here's what I need from each of you, and why it matters."

Clear communication doesn't eliminate fear, but it does channel anxiety into productive action instead of paralysis or procrastination.

5. Train before the Emergency Happens, Not During It

No firefighter shows up to their first wildfire without extensive training. We roll and bowl hose after hose. We practice. We study fire behavior. We run through scenarios and breakdowns. We make mistakes in controlled environments so we don't make them when lives (often our own) are at stake.

Sadly, I watch businesses approach AI like they're learning to fight fires while the flames surrounding them are already 20 meters high. They wait until competitive pressure forces their hand. Then they scramble to understand the software and tools, training their teams and implementing solutions simultaneously.

> *The decisions you make under panic are rarely strategic. Your ideas rushed under pressure are fragile, and teams learning under crisis conditions retain less and resist more.*

This approach guarantees a rough ride. The decisions you make under panic are rarely strategic. Your ideas rushed under pressure are fragile, and teams learning under crisis conditions retain less and resist more.

The organizations that will dominate the AI era are investing in training, experimentation, and capability-building right now. Not because they have a specific AI project on the roadmap but because they know that change is coming and they refuse to be unprepared.

Give your teams permission to experiment with AI tools. Create a space for learning and fund pilot projects. Accept that some experiments will fail because every mistake made in the training phase is a mistake you won't make when the stakes are high.

For Those Already in the Dead Man's Zone

I need to be direct about something uncomfortable. Some of you reading this are already in the dead man's zone. The AI fire has already traveled much farther and much faster than you thought it would. Your competitors are leveraging tools you don't understand, and new talent is moving toward organizations that embrace AI. Sadly, customers are starting to expect capabilities you can't deliver — yet.

If this is you, I understand the temptation to panic or give up. But here's what firefighting has taught me: **even in the worst situations, focused, disciplined action cures fear.**

When you're caught in a bad position, you have three options:

Option 1: Prepare for Burnover

In firefighting, when you're caught and can't escape, you go into a burnover procedure. Sheltering inside our trucks is a last resort. Hopefully, it keeps you alive until the fire passes.

The business equivalent is simplification and focus. Stop trying to do everything. Identify the 20% of your business that drives 80% of the value. Protect that core ruthlessly, then automate or eliminate everything else. Use AI tools to compress your timelines and multiply output in your highest-value activities.

This won't win you the war, but it does buy you time to regroup and reposition.

Option 2: Head to Your Safety Zone

Sometimes there's a creek bed, a rocky outcrop, or an already-burned area (*the black*) that you can reach safely if you move quickly. It requires abandoning your current position and moving, but it's often the best option.

The business equivalent is a **strategic pivot.** If AI is consuming your current market position, look for other spaces where you can leverage your existing strengths in new ways. Don't fight to defend indefensible ground. Think safety first. Move to where you can win.

This can be terrifying because it means admitting your current strategy isn't viable, but survival beats pride every time.

Option 3: Call for Backup

Professional firefighters don't operate alone, and neither should business leaders when they're facing existential challenges. If you're in over your head, bring in experts who've navigated this problem before.

Leverage outside expertise aggressively. Consultants, part-time executives, and AI implementation partners are all investments that pay for themselves many times over through compressed learning and mistakes avoided.

This isn't admitting weakness. It's recognizing that speed matters more than ego, and sometimes the fastest path forward is to listen to someone else.

The Choice Every Leader Must Make

I opened this chapter talking about the dead man's zone in front of a wildfire. It's that critical space where the fire moves faster than you can escape. But there's something else firefighters know that applies perfectly to AI leadership:

The dead man's zone isn't where the fire is. It's where the fire is going.

Right now, AI might not seem like a big threat to your business. Your current methods still work. Revenue might be stable. Your teams are productive. Everything feels manageable.

But the fire is moving quickly. Research by the *Harvard Gazette*[4] shows that 28 percent of employed people already use AI at work, and that number is doubling year on year._Your competitors, or future competitors that don't even exist yet, are operating at a velocity and scale you can't anticipate.

The question isn't whether AI will transform your industry. The question is whether you're standing in the dead man's zone right now. Are you in the path of where the fire is headed — and you just don't realize it yet?

---

4   https://news.harvard.edu/gazette/story/2024/10/generative-ai-embraced-faster-than-internet-pcs/

You have three choices:

Choice 1: Get ahead of the Fire Line

Embrace AI leadership fully. Invest in learning, experimentation, and implementation. Try to position yourself and your organization where the fire can't reach you — because you've already moved to safer ground.

This requires courage, an investment of time and money, and the willingness to disrupt yourself before the market does it for you. It means making bets on technologies that aren't fully mature and training for scenarios you can't perfectly predict.

But it also means taking control. You dictate the pace and direction of change rather than having it pushed onto you.

Choice 2: Stay in the Dead Man's Zone

You acknowledge AI exists, but you hesitate to commit and end up watching competitors pull ahead. You get to study the technology from a distance and wait for more certainty, clearer ROI, and better conditions.

This is the most common choice, but it's also the most dangerous. It feels prudent not to act until you're sure, but in bad conditions, prudence becomes paralysis. By the time you're certain, you've already been burned.

Choice 3: Accept Being Burned

Consciously choose not to compete in this space. Accept that your growth will be limited, your relevance will diminish, and your competitive position will erode over time as you fall behind your competition.

For some businesses and leaders, this is actually the right strategic choice. Not everyone needs to be at the leading edge. Some markets will remain relatively insulated from AI disruption for years, so some careers can coast to retirement on their existing expertise.

But make this choice consciously, with your eyes open and an of understanding the full implications. *Please don't drift into obsolescence by accident.*

The View from the Fire Line

After 20 years fighting wildfires and 35 years riding technology waves, I can tell you this: the front line *is* where you want to be.

Not in the path of the fire — that's the dead man's zone — but right at the edge, where you can see what's coming, influence where it goes, and capitalize on the opportunities it creates. That's where the most rewarding work and results happen.

Yes, it requires vigilance. Yes, it demands continuous learning and adaptation. And yes, it means embracing uncertainty and occasional failure. But the alternative is watching from a distance as others capture opportunities, innovate at speeds you can't match, and build an advantage you can't overcome. That will be far more painful.

The discomfort of change is temporary, but the consequences of inaction last forever.

I've generated over 100 million website visitors and billions in sales for clients, not because I'm smarter than everyone else but because I've consistently chosen to position myself ahead of the fire line rather than in its path. I've adapted, reinvented, and repositioned myself through multiple technology revolutions. I've had to write off my own expertise and start learning from scratch more than once. Many times, to be honest. And I can tell you with absolute certainty what I've learned from both fighting fires and in boardrooms: the discomfort of change is temporary, but the consequences of inaction last forever.

We're living through the fastest technological adoption in human history. ChatGPT reached 800 million users in just two years — a milestone that took the internet decades to achieve. AI isn't coming. It's here, it's accelerating, and the dead man's zone is expanding every day.

The leaders who emerge from this era won't be those who had perfect strategies from day one. They'll be the ones who read the conditions, respected the change, positioned themselves strategically, and refused to stand in the path of the coming fire pretending it didn't exist.

Final Warning from the Fire Line

In firefighting, we have a saying: *The fire doesn't care about your plans.*

It doesn't matter how experienced you are, how well equipped your crew is, or how confident you feel. When conditions change, fire will do what fire does.

AI doesn't care about your plans either. It doesn't care about your current success, your market position, or your years of experience. It's moving with exponential acceleration, reshaping the world whether you're ready or not.

So, I'll leave you with the question every firefighter and every business leader must answer honestly:

Are you prepared for the fire, or are you standing in the dead man's zone?

Right now, you still have time to move. But that window is closing. The AI fire is traveling faster than most people realize, and the distance it will cover in the next five minutes is greater than the distance it has already covered.

The choice is yours but make it quickly.

Fire doesn't wait for anyone.

— Brad

About Brad

Brad Hauck stands at a unique intersection few leaders occupy: the front lines of both Australian bushfires and technological firestorms.

For over twenty years, Brad has served as an officer and volunteer rural firefighter in Australia, responding to hundreds of wildfires and emergencies. This frontline experience has profoundly shaped his understanding of exponential change, strategic positioning and survival under extreme conditions.

In parallel, he has spent twenty-five years navigating digital transformation as "Mr Web Marketing," generating over 100 million website visitors and billions in sales for clients. As a keynote speaker in 54+ countries and author of bestselling books AI Powered Profits and Micro Course Profits, he helps organizations understand that like wildfires, AI transformation moves exponentially.

Whether coordinating containing a bushfire or advising companies on AI & marketing strategy, Brad brings the same fundamental insight: leaders who survive accelerating change aren't those who react fastest to danger. They're the ones who anticipate movement and position themselves ahead of the fire line before the critical moment arrives.

Learn how Brad can help position your organisation ahead of the AI fire line at www.proficlix.com.au

As the day moves deeper into the realities of modern leadership, we arrive at a pivotal moment.

Because by now, it's clear that AI isn't coming — it's already here. Data is abundant. Dashboards are full. Insights are constant. And yet, many leaders feel less certain, not more.

Introducing Fiona Kearns, UK

Fiona Kearns invites us to explore what it truly means to lead with confidence in a data-driven world — without losing visibility, decisiveness, or humanity in the process. Drawing on her background as a business psychologist and former tech CEO, Fiona cuts through the noise to address the mindset shift leaders must make when information is everywhere and pressure is high.

This is not a chapter about becoming more technical. It's about becoming more grounded.

Fiona shows us how confident leadership today requires discernment, psychological safety, and the courage to stay human — even when the data is loud. Her insights help leaders balance analytics with intuition, speed with reflection, and certainty with curiosity.

If you've ever wondered how to stay steady, visible, and credible while navigating complexity and constant change, this chapter is for you.

CHAPTER ELEVEN

AI and the New Work Order

What AI Tools Are Being Used in the Workplace Today

Generative AI has gone mainstream for most people in the workplace, driven by easy-access tools available at no additional cost. There is little barrier to entry, and the tools can be used credibly without much tweaking.

Businesses across every sector—from construction to biopharma—are turning to AI to boost productivity. With tight margins and little room for error, especially in small and medium-sized enterprises, optimizing every possible advantage has become essential. It's no surprise, then, that organizations are embracing leading AI tools. Here's a snapshot of some of the most popular tools being used in workplaces today.

- Easy-access Gen AI tools, such as Microsoft Copilot and the free version of OpenAI's ChatGPT

- Note-taking tools such as Fathom, which record, transcribe, and summarize Zoom and Teams calls

- Canva, a graphic design platform used for presentations, websites, and more

Power users are individuals who work beyond basic AI tools and explore more advanced capabilities, often by investing in paid versions, which demonstrates a higher level of commitment. For example, as of the end of 2025, there were approximately one billion ChatGPT users, with about ten million paying for advanced options.[1][2] Other platforms favored by power users include:

- Text-to-video generators

- Zapier for automation

- Google Gemini (particularly popular in the U.S., and India).

In the U.S., ChatGPT leads the generative AI market with a 60.4% share, followed by Microsoft Copilot at 14.1% and Google Gemini at 13.5%.[3] Google Gemini usage is highest in the U.S. (63%) and India (15%).[4]

Workers across the globe are using AI and reaping the rewards. A colleague working in the health sector has transformed her workload investigating workplace complaints. One tedious and time-consuming task has been wading through the transcripts of meetings for evidence of suspected poor employee behaviour. AI has made it infinitely more manageable and significantly reduced her workload delivering value for money for the organisation and more job satisfaction for her as she gets to use her pertinent skills. Instead of

---

1   Exploding Topics. (2025). ChatGPT users.
https://explodingtopics.com/blog/chatgpt-users
2   Vincent, J. (2025). ChatGPT has hit 20 million paid subscribers. The Verge.
https://www.theverge.com/openai/640894/chatgpt-has-hit-20-million-paid-subscribers
3   https://firstpagesage.com/reports/top-generative-ai-chatbots/
4   https://enlyft.com/tech/products/google-gemini

dreading a task that takes hours, she is able to sense check the data and deliver a faster more efficient investigation.

However, not every A.I. tool is fully embraced. For example, as shift is happening regarding note taking devices in online meetings and I've seen an increase in events and meetings not permitting note takers to protect the privacy of a meeting particularly when held under Chatham House Rules to facilitate free speech and confidentiality at meetings. Overall, this seems like a very sensible approach and of course I recognise that for some people they're a helpful tool. Personally, I think that if you can't make the meeting, it's not a priority and that's ok. As a person who did turn up I feel it's disrespectful to those there to think that sending a notetaker is sufficient. Plus, I really wonder how many really go through the actual notes as I rarely do myself and strongly suspect I'm not alone. What do you think?

Who is Not Using AI?

Who are the people not using AI in the workplace today? Mostly, latecomers are made up of purists and environmentalists. While this may be a relatively small group, it is interesting to note what is currently influencing them:

Latecomers

People are often apologetic that they're not doing more in this space, but increasingly they are experimenting with AI after encouragement from colleagues who show how it can speed up processes, particularly when easy-access tools like Copilot are built into their office software. Notably, even apologetic non-users are quick to share *how* they are using AI in other parts of their organization or their lives outside of work. Often, however, even where individuals are not using AI themselves, their organization is embracing it in some form, such as administration, laboratory innovation, or legal documentation.

Purists: Use It or Lose It

Previously, there was a cohort of people (and I am sure some still exist) who intentionally chose not to embrace AI, citing its soullessness or a tendency toward laziness and cognitive atrophy. These are likely the same people who prefer paper maps to getting directions on their phones. Neither position is indefensible, but both increasingly appear to be fighting against a technological tsunami.

Environmentalists

There are also those who raise concerns about the environmental impact of AI, particularly the energy demands of training local large language models (LLLMs) and the huge costs of operating data centers. This will become more central as governments and public industry organizations respond to these concerns. They must be balanced against available national resources, with some governments, such as Ireland's, restricting the construction of new data centers due to their impact on the national grid.

8 Common Love/Hate Factors About Gen AI

Everyone has an opinion about AI regardless of whether they use it or not. Here are the most common comments doing the rounds lately.

1. **Personality transplant:** We love how easy it is to convert draft text into something more polished, but we hate when it turns it into something we just wouldn't ever say.

2. **Back to square 1:** We love how it takes our ideas and offers suggestions, but we get frustrated when we don't like the suggestions and end up reverting to what we had to begin with.

3. **Confusion**: We love that free versions of ChatGPT are available, but we hate the proliferation of versions and the lack of clarity about which one to choose. . In ChatGPT5 the options are clearer, version 5.2 offers: *Instant* = answers right away, *Thinking* = Thinks longer for better answers and *Auto=*

decides how long to think. You can choose earlier versions of ChatGPT but there's little reason to use it

4. **Same, same—but different:** We love that we can ask it anything but hate that asking the same question twice does not always produce the same answer. The lack of replicability really bugs me, although I recognize that's the hard-wired business psychologist in me. I take deep breaths to manage it. However, it doesn't make sense for a system or a person to give different answers to the exact same question without any other obvious variables so it's very frustrating. . This randomness has a name: stochasticity!

5. **Wrong answers:** We love that it always provides an answer but hate when it's wrong. This particularly worries us because we have to know enough to recognize when an answer is wrong; otherwise, you'd be spouting nonsense "And it's frustrating that wrong answers require repeated redirection." **Clever—or creepy:** We love when AI hears and actions what we say, such as "I'd better cut this bit out later," but it is creepy that it does that, and it makes us wonder what else is it doing without our explicit direction.

Wouldn't it be really weird if every time I asked you a question, you gave a different answer? This kind of randomness has a name: stochasticity!

---

6. **Work-shy users**: We love what AI can do, but we don't always want to invest the time required to optimize our use of it.

7. **Is it good or bad?** We love its potential but hate that we don't fully understand it yet.

AI Concerns for Leaders Today
Ethics, Transparency, and Workload

Leaders are cautious about using generative AI, while also seeing the benefit of using it for some aspects of work. The ability of AI to fast-track aspects of a proposal or generate new ideas is widely embraced. Concerns include submitting work produced solely by AI and the potential reputational damage this may cause. There are also concerns about AI-generated content being presented as an individual's personal work.

Workload Help: Useful, But What About Misrepresentation?

Transparency is another concern. People do not always make it clear that AI has been used, even though clues such as leaving in dashes or the inclusion of American English terminology for those who use UK English are a dead giveaway. We now wonder about authenticity if AI use is not openly declared.

These days, the use of em dashes and bullet points is often seen as a clear signal that AI is involved; however, they are legitimate and useful elements of written language. But mitigating that is a big thing. And can be done—as this sentence itself attempts to demonstrate.

Practical AI Guidance at Work

Will we move toward a place where content will go the way of foods and drinks such as Champagne? Only sparkling wine produced in that region of France can be labeled "champagne"; other sparkling wines have to be called something different, such as Crémant in France, Franciacorta and Prosecco in Italy, Cava in Spain, and Sekt in Germany.

Already, many people disclose whether AI was used in creating a document, image, or video as a way of aligning with their personal ethics. I can see how that could be useful and a fair warning. On the other hand, I don't routinely tell people when I have used spellcheck on my document, even though it can also alter text in meaningful ways. In many areas, the issue isn't black and white, and we must ask ourselves whether there is truly an appetite for this level of regulation.

Training Wheels

Organizations are concerned about how best to use AI as an enhancement for many areas of their business, while also worrying that overreliance may bypass their usual checks and common-sense judgment.

No Brainer

Discussions about AI often focus on its utility, but far less time is spent considering its impact on our creativity and thinking ability. More than a decade ago, a university lecturer friend of mine expressed concern about the lack of critical thinking skills among first-year students, many of whom arrived at university having been "spoon-fed" through secondary school. With education systems often prioritizing exam results over genuine learning, she felt overwhelmed trying to bridge that gap. Now we must ask: does AI further erode our critical thinking skills—and does that matter if AI can fill the gap for us? Most of us would agree that we still want to preserve our own curiosity, reasoning, and intellectual capacity. A recent MIT survey highlights this concern, revealing that brain power dropped by 47% following AI use.[5] This finding suggests we should be mindful of how we rely on AI in every aspect of life.

New Work Order

The world of work is shifting and evolving all the time. Higher levels of anxiety, a move to working from home, and an endless drive to be more productive prevail. Add to this a growing sense of disconnection from colleagues at work. Two questions come to mind as I ponder this:

5   MIT Media Lab. (2024). *Your brain on ChatGPT*. Research conducted by Nataliya Kos'mina.   https://www.media.mit.edu/publications/your-brain-on-chatgpt/

- Is AI improving connections at work?
- How can AI improve personal relationships at work?

Arguably, this is a separate subject, but I'm always interested in how we make work better, and these are two hot-button topics for leaders right now.

Bring Your Whole Self to Work

When particularly competent people join the workforce with high expectations of themselves, their colleagues, and their organization, disappointment ensues when progression feels slow and the reality fails to match the dream. It can seem unfair that progress doesn't unfold as they were promised, and senior leaders may find themselves helping employees adjust to reality—another demand on already limited time!

Team leaders often encourage workers to bring in personal problems—mental, financial, or otherwise—and attempt to resolve them at work. Noble and well intentioned, but the burden on leaders is high, and it raises the question of where to draw the line. It's not always clear. Leaders already have significant demands on their time and often aren't resourced to manage this shift in expectations. Not all organizations can justify having an on-call or permanent counselor. Complaints to HR have increased in recent years, and while AI tools that support or equip leaders are most welcome, I firmly believe that much of this increase reflects a deeper workplace disconnection that requires personal solutions rather than impersonal technology. But could AI tools actually facilitate better personal connection?

DEI Backlash

Notwithstanding the "bring your whole self to work" shift, a backlash against Diversity, Equity and Inclusion (DEI) is emerging in some quarters, with critics arguing that these efforts have gone too far. Court cases and government actions have shifted the tone of the debate away from deeper conversations and toward more entrenched viewpoints. It's hardly novel to observe that division, rather than collaboration, makes better news.

Algorithms can present powerful echo chambers, delivering more of what we already believe to be correct. Great for money-making websites; not great for societies. And it poses challenges for organizations that want to do the right thing—a hallmark of many hardworking leaders in small and medium-sized businesses. What happens when the backlash goes online?

A.I. is a Resource

In the realm of a new work order as we move beyond the hype, A.I. is being more readily recognised as a resource to be deployed in organisations. In January 2026, CEO of McKinsey & Company, Bob Sternfels, shared that the firm has 60,000 employees, with 25,000 of them being AI agents. At first, that might seem a bit shocking and it highlights where organisations have positioned AI for their business. It's happening now not in the future.[6]

As a resource, it is more readily recognised that it should subject to the same checks and balances as we would other resources. More questions concerning quality and security of the data is coming to the fore with more focus on data governance within organisations.

Increasingly, there is a concern on where data of all kinds are stored with concerns in particular on U.S. locations which have less regulation and increasing geopolitical concerns. The sensitivities have become more pronounced with organisations actively seeking "Digital Sovereignty" in the form of local options to address those concerns.

Similarly on an individual level, we can see these issues come

---

6   Ref: https://www.theregister.com/2025/11/13/gartner_cio_cloud_sovereignty/?utm_source=chatgpt.com

through as people seeking alternatives to the socalled 'hyper scalers' Amazon, Microsoft and Google. It can be challenging to find local alternatives that meet the same level of service and price point. It will be interesting to follow how these impact the cost and organisational needs in terms of A.I.

Governments are concerned with advances that are not good for society such as Grok AI creating sexualised deepfake images and they are taking action accordingly. Lack of regulation has its downside very clearly and can't go unfettered. Regulation will become a fact of life for AI even if legislation will take time to catch-up. However, there has been a backlash against regulation that hampers economic growth and Draghi's report on EU competitiveness makes it very clear that the focus will be on aligning regulation with growth.

New World Order AI: Do No Harm

In medicine the concept of 'Do no Harm' is well known ethical principle. What if we were to embrace this principle in A.I.

The new world order may look different, but in many ways it remains similar to the old one. We need to remain vigilant about advances that advantage or disadvantage particular groups. After all, history is written by the winners, and even that narrative is con-tested, as those defeated in battle have not always had access to edu-cation and the opportunity to record their views. It's easy to take our 21st-century privileges for granted, and that shields us from some of the harsher realities experienced by others.

AI presents many opportunities to improve our lives, but we need to be mindful of the broader impact and less accepting of changes that simply don't impact us directly. The world has always benefited from strong leadership, and advances in AI will require it just as much. Some of that leadership may simply be paying attention and holding systems to account. Would it be useful to insist, first and foremost, that AI does no harm?

— *Fiona*

About Fiona

Fiona Kearns, Certified Business Psychologist and former tech CEO, works across IT, non-profit and commercial sectors to build leadership capability for investment, innovation and growth. With a strong IT background, she brings a critical, practical perspective on AI's workplace impact.

Fiona holds advanced qualifications in Business Psychology, including BPS registration for psychometrics and accreditations in Neuroscience, Psychological Safety, Decision-Making, and Strengths. As the creator of CEO Confident, she empowers women to lead and helps organisations harness the power of diverse leadership. Her work combines deep psychological insight with practical leadership development through consulting, coaching and training.

Kearns Consultancy equips executive teams to think, communicate and lead differently for next-level results. Fiona helps client organisations turn brilliant technical experts into confident people managers who can give *clear, high impact feedback, tackle conflict early, and keep teams motivated through constant change.* The outcomes are commercial and clear: lower attrition, stronger wellbeing, and a measurable lift in productivity.

For more information please visit:
https://kearnsconsultancy.com/ai

Reviewing the Voices That Shaped This Conference

Connect, Lead, Succeed 2

Before we close the room, it's worth pausing to acknowledge the voices that shaped this conversation — each bringing a distinct perspective, lived experience, and leadership lens to the day.

Harriet L. Russell opens the conference by taking us inward. Her chapter reminds us that leadership begins with self-awareness, presence, and cultural intelligence. Drawing on Japanese wisdom and decades of global experience, Harriet reframes leadership as something we embody rather than perform — inviting leaders to slow down, listen more deeply, and lead from alignment rather than urgency.

Kim Liddell grounds leadership firmly in the real world. Through stories forged underground — quite literally — she shows how credibility is earned through consistency, responsibility, and showing up when it matters. Her chapter is a powerful reminder that confidence is not claimed, but built, one careful step at a time, often where no one is watching.

Sarah Morse challenges us to expand our definition of courage. Her chapter introduces the Courage Equation — connecting courage, purpose, action, and impact — and asks leaders to consider the legacy their decisions create. Drawing from humanitarian work and systemic change, Sarah reminds us that leadership is always ethical work, whether we acknowledge it or not.

Dr. Suresh Verghis brings leadership into the space where it actually happens: conversation. His chapter explores conversational agility as a core leadership capability — showing how trust, adaptability, and curiosity in dialogue shape culture, innovation, and outcomes. This is leadership practiced moment by moment, word by word.

Claudia Cimenti invites us into the often-avoided space of friction. Rather than smoothing over tension, she shows leaders how to stay present in it — transforming discomfort into clarity and conflict into momentum. Her chapter reframes friction not as failure, but as one of leadership's most powerful growth signals.

Bronwyn Reid grounds leadership in responsibility and risk. Through compelling examples, she demonstrates how leadership decisions ripple outward — impacting trust, reputation, and long-term viability. Her chapter is a reminder that leadership is not just about what is legal or efficient, but about what is ethical, sustainable, and worthy of trust.

Ravin Souvendra Papiah rounds out the leadership session of the conference by bringing communication, leadership, and influence together. His chapter focuses on how ideas move from intention to impact — and how leaders can communicate with clarity, credibility, and purpose in complex environments. Ravin leaves us with a sense of integration and forward motion.

Libby Edmonds recentres us on emotional intelligence in a fast-moving world. Her chapter highlights the human skills that remain essential — self-awareness, empathy, regulation, and connection — especially as technology accelerates. Libby reminds us that emotionally intelligent leadership is not optional; it is foundational.

Rainer Petek reframes the human-AI relationship entirely. Using the metaphor of a rope team, he shows how humans and AI can move forward together — safely, intentionally, and with shared responsibility. His chapter positions AI not as a replacement, but as a partner guided by human judgment and leadership.

Brad Hauck brings urgency and realism to the AI conversation. Drawing on firefighting and digital leadership, his chapter challenges leaders to act before crisis forces their hand. Brad's message is clear: preparation, experimentation, and capability-building must happen before the flames are at the door.

Fiona Kearns closes the conference by addressing AI and the New Work Order. She brings psychological insight and commercial realism to how AI is reshaping leadership expectations and workplace dynamics. Fiona challenges leaders to engage thoughtfully

— building confidence, capability, and clarity as roles evolve. Her closing message is powerful: technology may redefine work, but leadership maturity determines whether that change strengthens or destabilises organisations.

And finally, this book itself — as a collective voice — reminds us that leadership is not a single skill, framework, or moment. It is a practice. One shaped by who we are, how we connect, and the tools we choose to use responsibly.

Where Leadership Goes from Here

BY DIXIE MARIA CARLTON

As we come to the close of this book, imagine us back in the conference room.

The final sessions have wrapped up.

Notes are scribbled in margins.

A few ideas have landed more deeply than expected.

This is always my favourite moment at any conference — not because everything has been answered, but because something has shifted.

That's what **Connect, Lead, Succeed 2** was designed to do.

Not to overwhelm you with information.

Not to convince you to adopt someone else's version of leadership.

But to create space — for reflection, recalibration, and more intentional choices about how you lead in a rapidly changing world.

What This Book Has Been About

Throughout Book 2, two conversations have run side by side.

The first was about **leadership** — the inner work, the courage, the conversations, the friction, and the responsibility that comes with influence. We explored leadership as something practiced daily, not declared occasionally. Something human, imperfect, and deeply consequential.

The second was about **capability** — particularly Artificial Intelligence — and how leaders can engage with powerful tools without outsourcing judgment, ethics, or accountability.

And here's the thread that ties them together:

The more powerful our tools become, the more intentional our leadership must be.

AI may change how we work.
But leadership determines *why*, *how*, and *to what end*.

The contributors in this book didn't offer you shortcuts. They offered you perspective. Lived experience. Hard-won insight. And, in many cases, permission — to pause, to rethink, and to lead more deliberately.

Before We Close the Room...

Before we stack the chairs and turn off the lights, I want to leave you with something practical — the kind of thing you might jot down at the end of a conference and return to later.

Consider this your **Leadership Takeaway Checklist** from *Connect, Lead, Succeed 2.*

Not as rules.

But as reminders.

The Connect, Lead, Succeed Leadership Checklist

Before you move on, ask yourself:

- ☐ Am I leading from clarity — or from habit?
- ☐ Do my actions consistently reflect the values I say matter most?
- ☐ Where do I need to slow down before I scale up?
- ☐ Am I willing to have the conversations I've been postponing?
- ☐ Do I create space for productive friction — or avoid discomfort altogether?
- ☐ Am I using technology to extend my thinking — or to avoid it?
- ☐ Where does human judgment need to stay firmly in the loop?
- ☐ Have I defined what success actually means for me in this season?
- ☐ Am I leading in a way I'd be proud to be remembered for?
- ☐ What is one small, intentional change I can make this week?

You don't need to answer all of these today.

But leadership has a way of circling back to the questions we ignore.

The Real Invitation

If there is one message I hope you carry forward from this book, it's this:

Leadership is not static — and neither are you.

The best leaders I know are not the ones who have everything figured out. They are the ones who remain curious, grounded, and willing to evolve — even as expectations rise and the pace accelerates.

This book does not ask you to lead harder.

It asks you to lead *truer*.

To reconnect with what matters.

To choose tools with discernment.

And to remember that impact is not accidental — it is shaped by the decisions we make repeatedly, often quietly, over time.

Closing the Conference

So as we close this chapter — and this book — imagine the final applause.

Not for perfection.
But for participation.

For showing up to the conversation.
For staying open.
For being willing to lead in a world that doesn't offer simple answers anymore.

Thank you for spending this time with us.

Thank you for leaning into the questions.

And most of all, thank you for the leadership you take back with you when you close this book.

The conference may be ending — but the work continues.

Until the next conversation,

keep connecting.

Keep leading.

And keep succeeding — in ways that truly matter.

— Dixie

*We hope you have enjoyed reading this book and have been
inspired by the many exceptional speakers and authors
featured here.*

*The **Virtual Speakers Association International** is a
supporting organization offering networking, development
and events for people around the world who are professional
speakers, trainers and facilitators of learning. If you would
like to learn more about us and how we may be able to
support your journey as a professional speaker, or if you
would like to engage with any of our speakers for your next
event any where in the world, please visit us today at:*

www.vsainternational.org

Want More?

Your conference doesn't end here - we've got more to share.

Maybe you're interested in being part of one of our **next books** in this series or **sponsorship opportunities**?

What about turning your next industry conference into a **CONFERENCE IN A BOOK**™ *special edition*?

Scan the **QR code** or visit
www.indieexpertspublishing.com/conferenceinabook

➤ Get exclusive bonus resources (*Access Password:* **CIAB#125**)

➤ Be the first to know about upcoming volumes in the series

➤ Access tools, guides, and insights you won't find anywhere else

Stay connected. Keep learning. Keep leading.

Conference in a Book™

Proudly brought to you by Indie Experts Publishing